MW01533968

PRAIS

"This book shows
emissions wherever they have influence. It's well-
researched, clearly written, and informative. It's nothing
like what I expected. It was a real breath of fresh air."

— *Greg Ballard*, 48th mayor of Indianapolis; retired Lt. Col. U.S. Marines;
author of Small Unit Leadership *and* Less Oil or More Caskets: The
National Security Argument for Moving Away From Oil

"In *Carbon Neutral Indiana: A Practical Guide to Climate
Optimism*, Daniel Poynter is anything but neutral. His
pragmatic approaches are clever, sometimes funny and very
convincing. This book is an essential primer for everyone
wishing to implement climatic solutions and help the world
avoid a possible devastating environmental tragedy."

— *Mickey Maurer*, Chairman of the Board of IBJ Corporation and
The National Bank of Indianapolis; former President of the Indiana Economic
Development Corp.; former Indiana Secretary of Commerce

"Discussions about climate change have almost exclusively
focused on the problem, diminishing the prospect of
hope, innovation and practical solutions. This book
highlights the stories of entrepreneurs who are driving
change and creating a future of lower carbon, economic
growth, and continued human flourishing."

— *Kristian Andersen*, Co-Founder & Partner, High Alpha

"A few people are changing how Indiana thinks about climate
change. Daniel Poynter is one. *Carbon Neutral Indiana: A
Practical Guide to Climate Optimism* is all about solutions and
opportunities. It provides a roadmap that can benefit all Hoosiers."

— *Jim Merritt*, President, JWM Consulting Corp.;
Indiana State Senator; Indiana Bicentennial Commission

"To truly spur action, just inspiration and education are not
enough – we must also empower individuals and make them feel
that their actions are part of a bigger collective. The personal
empowerment that people will get from this book will surely
spark action towards solutions in their own communities."

— *Colleen Marciel Rosales, PhD*, Atmospheric and Indoor Air Pollution
Chemist with the University of California

"Instead of doomsday forecasts and constant front-page gloom, we need a vision of a clean, sustainable future. For those of us feeling overwhelmed and unsure about the climate crisis, this book will get us off our duff and into the game."

—*Dr. F. Ryan Prall, MD*, Retinologist

"Daniel makes the science, engineering, and policy approachable by providing both immediate ideas for any community to implement and inspiration for entrepreneurial minds to create new technologies and economic opportunities."

— *Landon Gary Young, PhD*, Venture Capitalist and Executive Director of Entrepreneurial Programming at Elevate Ventures; PhD Ecological Science and Engineering

"This book is full of good resources and great local stories, one of which is sure to inspire you to take similar actions. Is another town doing something needed or possible in your town? Did someone else take on a task, not knowing if they were capable or whether they'd be successful? We are all important and necessary in the face of this challenge."

— *Molly O'Donnell*, volunteer with Earth Care Bloomington

"So much about the climate crisis is presented to us on a seemingly intractable national or global scale. The truth is there are small, concrete things that Hoosiers can do to be a part of climate solutions. It's time that we flip the script on climate from crisis to opportunity, and this book moves us in that direction."

— *Andrew Gouty*, CEO of Science & Magic

"Daniel Poynter's enthusiasm for creative climate action is palpable and infectious, and his efforts to spread the good news of pragmatic solutions offered in Indiana gives us hope for our children and grandchildren. The book begs the question at the end of each chapter – "Can I do this?" My resounding response is: "YES!""

— *John Mundell*, CEO, Mundell & Associates; Global Director of the Catholic Church's climate Laudato Si Action Platform

CARBON NEUTRAL INDIANA

a practical guide to
climate optimism

FIRST EDITION

by

Daniel Scott Poynter

Copyright © 2022 by Daniel Scott Poynter.

All rights are reserved. No part of this publication may be reproduced, distributed, or transmitted in any form or by any means, including photo-copying, recording, or other electronic or mechanic methods, without the prior written permission of the publisher, except in the case of brief quota-tions embodied in critical reviews and certain other noncommercial uses permitted by copyright law. For permission requests, write to the publisher, addressed "Attention: Permissions Coordinator," at the address below.

**carbon
neutral**
INDIANA

Carbon Neutral Indiana
PO Box 20779
Indianapolis IN, 46220
317-721-4587
carbonneutralindiana.org

ORDERING INFORMATION

QUANTITY SALES Special discounts are available on quantity purchases by corporations, associations, and others. For details, contact the "Special Sales Department" at the address above.

INDIVIDUAL SALES This publication is available for purchase online directly at **317-721-4587** and **carbonneutralindiana.org**

For adoption in college textbooks / course design, please use the contact information above.

Printed in the United States.

CATALOGING DATA
Name: Poynter, Daniel Scott, author.
Title: Carbon Neutral Indiana: A Practical Guide to Climate Optimism.
Description: First edition. | Summary: "This book offers stories of people reducing carbon emissions in Indiana, how-to guides, relevant organiza-tions, and legislation." — provided by publisher.
Subjects: climate change | global warming | Indiana

First edition

BOOK DESIGN Rachel Leigh
COPYEDITORS Anne Laker, Lucas Bleyle
COVER DESIGN Brandon Schaaf

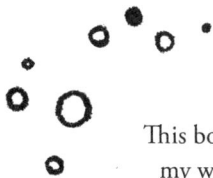

This book is dedicated to
my wife Cait Poynter,
and to our future children
and grandchildren.

"For that one fraction of a second,
you were open to options you
had never considered. That is
the exploration that awaits you.
Not mapping stars and studying
nebulae, but charting the unknown
possibilities of existence."

— Q, Star Trek

If your eyes sparkled when
you read that, this book is
also dedicated to you.

This book is a practical manual for learning about and taking action on climate, starting from wherever you are today. Think of it as a field guide.

WONDERING WHERE TO START?

Youth! Flip to page *73*.

Educators, check out the stories on pages *23* and *33*.

Working people & retirees, you might start with pages *63* and *77*.

Elected officials, get inspired with the stories on pages *21*, *55*, and *79*.

Contents

Preface *8*   Acknowledgments *10*   Introduction *14*

ELECTRICITY *17*
Saving $30,000 with Residential Solar *19*
City Finances Energy-Efficient Buildings *21*
How Schools Are Saving Millions of Dollars *23*
Supplemental Resources *26*

FOOD, AGRICULTURE & LAND USE *31*
School Rescues Wasted Food *33*
Annual Event Celebrates Plant-Rich Lifestyle *35*
Supplemental Resources *36*

INDUSTRY *39*
Turning Sewage and Grease into Energy *41*
Recycling Urban Trees into Art *43*
Supplemental Resources *45*

TRANSPORTATION & BUILDINGS *49*
Ordinance Limits New Gas Stations *51*
Bringing Electric Transportation to Central Indiana *53*
Town Saves Money With White Roofs *55*
Supplemental Resources *57*

CARBON SINKS *61*
Man Plants 80,000 Trees Over 30 Years *63*
Capturing All of Indiana's Emissions *65*
Supplemental Resources *67*

ENABLING CONDITIONS *71*
Climate-Themed Little Free Libraries *73*
Mother Nurtures Environmental Community *75*
The Most Powerful Climate Solution of All *77*
Michigan City Creates Emissions Baseline *79*
Supplemental Resources *81*

Conclusion *85*   More Resources *87*

Discussion Questions *89*   Crossword Puzzle *92*

Preface

"Throughout my lifetime, politicians and pundits have constantly moaned about terrifying problems facing America … The prophets of doom have overlooked the all-important factor that is certain: human potential is far from exhausted, and the American system for unleashing that potential – a system that has worked wonders for over two centuries despite frequent interruptions for recessions and even a Civil War – remains alive and effective."

— Warren Buffet

I love Indiana. My parents raised me in a small town near Fort Wayne. Some of my favorite memories were playing baseball (especially the chatter: "Hey batter, batter… swing!"), riding our bicycles over homemade ramps until we crashed, staying up late at sleepovers to tell stories, listening with my father to AM radio, and of course, learning that school was canceled because of snow.

After graduating from Purdue University, I worked as a web developer and traveled the world as a digital nomad, even studying in Israel. Every time I land at the Indianapolis International Airport, I hum "Back Home Again in Indiana." This is where my wife and I will raise our children. I couldn't imagine living anywhere else.

In 2018, I learned that my grandchildren probably won't see a coral reef. Coral reefs are dying. The carbon dioxide we emit doesn't just stay in the air. The ocean absorbs about half of it. This makes the water acidic, killing the coral. How could I help? I took a year off to interview 300 people working on the environment, and I learned that half of the emissions in the U.S. come from just 10 states. Indiana is one. So in 2020, I created the nonprofit Carbon Neutral Indiana to grow a nonpartisan, pragmatic community of Hoosiers implementing climate solutions. We're concerned about the environment, but we're also pro-human and pro-growth. We're for free minds and free markets, for bottom-up innovation.

There's so much to learn. So in the past two years, I've interviewed 600 more people, including 100 for this book. I've interviewed the entire innovation pipeline, from scientists to Fortune 500 executives. For climate change, the pipeline works like this: scientists discover ways to reduce emissions, engineers turn those discoveries into inventions, and entrepreneurs market these as new products. Finally, Fortune 500 executives buy these products to become more competitive and profitable, which decarbonizes their companies. This profitability incentivizes investors to fund even more discovery and innovation.

And then there's society more generally. I've talked with elected officials of both parties at the city, state, and federal levels, who want to do the right thing for climate, but need us to build political will for them. I've spoken with nonprofit leaders who are building that political will. I've met working professionals like doctors, architects, farmers, and small business owners who want to volunteer a few hours after they put the kids to bed. And I've learned from retired Baby Boomers looking for meaningful ways to invest their remaining years.

For the past four years I've had my ear to the ground. What's special about Indiana? And how can we help solve one of this century's major challenges? This book amplifies a few success stories, but there are so many more to come. I hope this book is just the first edition of many. Will the next edition include your story?

Daniel Scott Poynter
Carbon Neutral Indiana
July 2022, Indianapolis, Indiana

Acknowledgments

I drew inspiration from *Project Drawdown* by Paul Hawken, *Centered* by Katie Pyzyk, *Whole Earth Catalog* by Stewart Brand, Gerry Dick at *Inside INdiana Business*, Nate Feltman and Mickey Maurer at the *Indianapolis Business Journal*, and *Explore Sustainable Indiana* by John Gibson.

Thank you to Harini Radhakrishnan, who contributed as a summer research assistant while pursuing her degree in Industrial Engineering from Purdue University. Thank you to Chris Powers and George Gemelas for meeting regularly during this book's creation, and to the advisory board who reviewed early drafts:

Greg Collins	Jacob Jewell	Chris Powers
Addie Farris	Tyler Kanczuzewski	Dr. Ryan Prall, MD
Zach Garcia	Caroline Nellis	Susan Schlag
Andrew Gouty	Molly O'Donnell	John Smillie
Marcia Hopkins	Cait Poynter	Mac Williams

Thank you to Anne Laker and Lucas Bleyle for copyediting, Rachel Leigh for designing the interior, and Brandon Schaaf for creating the cover. Thank you to David Harting for working his software magic.

Thank you to those who supported this book financially as of August 1, 2022. Your gifts helped to publish and distribute copies to leaders throughout Indiana.

Colleen Altschul	Louis S. Hensley Jr. Family Foundation, Inc.	Andrew Pappas
Erin Argyilan		Jamie Poloncak
Jan Black	Marcia Hopkins	Dr. Ryan Prall, MD
Jesse Brown	Andie Jahnz-Davis	Dorothy Reilly
Matt Courtney	Tyler Kanczuzewski	Katina Rivera
Alex Decker	Benjamin Keele	Colleen Rosales, PhD
Addie Farris	Greg Kempf	Joseph Sauer
Rebeca Gonzalez	Dexter & Patricia McCormick Family Foundation	Lamica Simmons
Andrew Gouty		John Smillie
Dr. Anne Greist, MD	Pam Michel	Sarah Stelzner
Jim Grimes	Tina Mills	Phil Teague
Steve Grossi	Nancy Moldenhauer	Fran Tuite
Mike Gunderloy	Erin Moodie	Sarah Vise
Beth Hannon	Brad Mueller	Stephanie von Hirschberg
Karrie Harbart	Molly O'Donnell	Roseann Woodka
Daphne Harris	Kelvin Okamoto	Brian Will
Laura Henderson	Daniel Overbey	

Special thanks to **Dawn Slack**, whose presentation on invasive species at North United Methodist Church in Indianapolis woke me up to environmental challenges. And to **Josh & Cara Bach**, for being the first carbon neutral household in Indiana, and to the over 200 other households and businesses certified carbon neutral through Carbon Neutral Indiana.

Finally, thank you to the many who granted interviews in the past few years. Here are some of them:

Kristian Andersen *High Alpha*
Topher Anderson *Citizens' Climate Lobby*
Paul Annee *Indianapolis City Council*
Barbara Backler *Retired educator*
Josh Bain *Indianapolis City Council*
Greg Ballard *Former Mayor of Indianapolis*
John Barth *Indianapolis City Council*
Ethan Bledsoe *Student*
Tom Bogenshutz *Tri-State Creation Care*
John Bohlman *HawkenAQ*
Vicki Bohlsen *Bohlsen Group*
Sarah Bowman *IndyStar*
Mike Braun *Indiana Senator*
Alison Brown *Indianapolis City Council*
Sam Bryan *GIS Professional*
Dwight Burlingame *Lilly Family School of Philanthropy*
Crista Carlino *Indianapolis City Council*
Deborah Chubb *Indiana Women's Action Movement, Inc.*
Mark Clayton *Citizens' Climate Lobby*
Lauren Clemens *City of Bloomington Office of Sustainability*
Casey Cotton *Storehouse Ventures*
Kacey Crane *Indiana Conservative Alliance for Energy*
Clayton De Fur *Herbert Simon Family Foundation*
Will Ditzler *Riverbirch Executive Advsiors*
Erika Dowell *The Lilly Library*
Jason DuPont *Lochmueller Group*
Lori Ecker *Citizens' Climate Lobby*
Beth Edwards *Indiana Environmental Reporter*
Kevin Ellett *Carbon Solutions LLC*
Greg Enas *Innovatov LLC*

Adrianna Farris *Eco Fest Fort Wayne*

Doug Fasick *Fort Wayne Utilities*

Eli Franklin *Student*

Bennett Fuson *EDP Renewables*

Zach Garcia *Wesselman Woods Land Trust*

Kerri Garvin *Greater Indiana Clean Cities, Inc.*

George Gemelas *Students for a Carbon Dividend*

Anthony Gillund *Purdue University*

George Giltner *Tech Point Youth Foundation*

Paul Goldman *Regal Beloit Corporation*

Ashley Gray *Richmond High School*

Derek Gray *Eli Lilly and Company*

Dr. Anne Greist *Indiana Hemophilia and Thrombosis Center*

Michael-Paul Hart *Indianapolis City Council*

Chris Haynes *Indiana University*

Scott Hensley *Louis S. Hensley Jr. Family Foundation, Inc.*

Kelly Hipskind *Sun FundED*

Leslie Hurst *Boy Scouts of America*

Tyler Kanczuzewski *Inovateus Solar*

Greg Kempf *Citizens' Climate Lobby*

Bryn Keplinger *City of Huntington*

Jeremy Kranowitz *Keep Indianapolis Beautiful*

Jason Larrison *Indianapolis City Council*

Mickey Maurer *The National Bank of Indianapolis*

Jessica McCormick *Indianapolis City Council*

Joe McGuinness *Avenew, Inc*

Mo McReynolds *Indianapolis Office of Sustainability*

Jim Merritt *Former State Senator*

Don Miller *Indianapolis Parks*

Alexander Mingus *Indiana Catholic Conference*

Allyson Mitchell *Circular Indiana*

Nancy Moldenhauer *Michigan City Sustainability Commission*

Faye Moore *Indiana Department of Corrections*

Matt Moore *Ball State University*

Caroline Nellis *Citizens' Climate Lobby*

Joanna Nixon *Efroymson Fund*

Daniel Overbey *Ball State University*

Andrew Pappas *Indiana Department of Environmental Management*

Alice Pawley *Purdue University*

Lindsey Payne *Purdue University*

Stephen Perkins *Faith in Place*

Jodi Perras *Sierra Club*

Jackie Phillips *Keep Our Village Clean*

Isabel Piedmont-Smith *Bloomington City Councilor*

Jim Poyser *Earth Charter Indiana*

Dr. Ryan Prall, MD *Associated Vitreoretinal and Uveitis Consultants*

Pam Pranger *Climate advisor to Mayor of Huntington*

Brian Presnell *Indy Urban Hardwood*

Aaron Rozzi *Boston Consulting Group*

Enrique Sainz *Indiana Environmental Reporter*

Karl Schneider *IndyStar*

Stephanie Schuck *Environmental Education Association of Indiana*

Paul Seidler *Evergreen Climate Innovations*

Audra Shock *Hinkle Creek Elementary*

Julie D. Singer *Raymond James & Associates*

John Smillie *Citizens' Climate Lobby*

Alex Smith *International Society of Sustainability Professionals*

Dr. Sarah Stelzner *Eskenazi Health*

Mark Stoops *Former State Senator*

Heather Swinney *Citizens' Climate Lobby*

Gene Tempel *Lilly Family School of Philanthropy*

Drew Tharp *Energy Systems Network*

Niesha Ward *Indiana Department of Workforce Development*

Leslie Webb *Carmel Green Initiative*

Kevin Whited *City of Carmel*

Brian Will *The Ohio State University*

Mac Williams *Licensed LEED AP*

Ben Wrightsman *Energy Systems Network*

Alison Zajdel *Stamm Koechlein Family Foundation*

Larry Zimmer *No Place Like Home*

Acknowledgment here does not imply endorsement of this book.

Introduction

It's easy to get overwhelmed by climate change. We can use an insight from Stephen Covey. In his classic book, *The 7 Habits of Highly Effective People*, Covey describes the Circle of Concern and the Circle of Influence. Many are concerned about matters outside their control, like recession or nuclear war. Focusing on issues like these can paralyze us with anxiety. But there are also things we *can* influence — like what media we allow into our minds, and which people we spend time with. When we choose to focus on these issues, a funny thing happens: we achieve small successes. These create a sense of possibility. Then we achieve more successes. This creates a positive feedback loop and momentum. We become more confident. We remember our power to shape this world. Our Circle of Influence expands.

With this insight in mind, let's start with the big goal. The largest assembly of scientists in human history is called the Intergovernmental Panel on Climate Change. They say the entire world needs to be carbon neutral by 2050. This means reducing our emissions and balancing out whatever remains by removing them. Hence the term *net-zero*.

How can we help the world become carbon neutral? This book is inspired by *Drawdown: The Most Comprehensive Plan Ever Proposed to Reverse Global Warming*, a list of the most effective climate solutions in the world. While Project Drawdown lays out a powerful global plan for addressing climate change, it lacks the local specificity to be actionable in Indiana. So I identified the solutions relevant to Indiana, interviewed Hoosiers implementing them, and collected resources to help you realize them wherever you have influence — your household, organization, or city. This book has three purposes:

INSPIRE. Nobody believed it was possible to run a four-minute mile, but Roger Bannister did it. Then, so did 37 others, because they knew it was possible. I hope the 60 or so true stories about Hoosiers reducing emissions are equally inspiring.

EDUCATE. Windmills and solar panels are just the tip of the iceberg. Project Drawdown identified dozens of other climate solutions. They also calculated their potential impact in two different scenarios by assessing how many gigatons of carbon dioxide or equivalents (Gt CO_2e) will be prevented or reduced. I averaged these results, and included them at the beginning of each chapter to give context to each solution.

ACTIVATE. Each story has a how-to guide so you can implement the solution. Each chapter includes a directory of organizations, what they can help you achieve, and their contact information. 51 organizations total. Chapters also include 29 relevant bills that you can research further, using the Indiana General Assembly's website (`iga.in.gov`).

1

WHY READ THIS BOOK?

This book shows how the climate movement can welcome both liberals and conservatives. Climate used to be nonpartisan. I could quote Ronald Reagan, George H. W. Bush, or George W. Bush. Here's Margaret Thatcher in 1984:

> "… the threat to our world comes not only from tyrants and their tanks. It can be more insidious though less visible. The danger of global warming is as yet unseen, but real enough for us to make changes and sacrifices, so that we do not live at the expense of future generations."

Yet most conservatives, and even some moderate liberals, don't feel comfortable in the climate movement today. Why? I think there are two main reasons.

First, the far left politicized climate by grouping it together with controversial social issues. I think they were well-meaning and tried to create a big tent of several political factions, but wise and decent people disagree about those social issues. Climate is too important to politicize.

The second reason has to do with "solution aversion," a concept from behavioral psychology. This explains how people deny a problem exists when they are opposed to the perceived solutions. The perceived solutions in this case have not been good. Much of the public thinks the only way to address climate change is by increasing the size of government. That's not true. This book highlights climate solutions that are compatible with the American way of life. Local, bottom-up innovation, guided by light, intelligent regulation like a price on carbon. When everyone feels included in the climate movement, the movement can benefit from everyone's gifts.

2 **This book can help us strengthen democracy.** A recent poll found a majority of young Europeans think authoritarian states are more effective than democracies when dealing with climate change. If a tyrant promises a solution to climate, will these young people forsake democracy? Young people need to know that democracies and the free market can respond to environmental challenges effectively. If not, tyrants may seize the opportunity to fortify their power while forsaking our planet.

3 **This book shows how we can save lives.** Researchers at Yale found that over 50% of Hoosiers are "worried" about climate. This is most acute in young people. Between 2007 and 2018, the rate of suicide among people aged 10 to 24 increased 60%. People are tired of feeling overwhelmed with no sense of control. Despair kills, but we can engender hope simply by showing a realistic path to a better life. People are looking for the specific, concrete climate solutions in this book. I believe this can save lives.

SUPPLEMENTARY RESOURCES can be found at CarbonNeutralIndiana.org/book. This companion website includes larger directory of organizations, video interviews, and links to sources throughout the book. It's also where you can submit resources for the next edition.

 **FEEDBACK** I want to hear from you. What did you think of the book? How can the next one be better? When you provide feedback, I'll send you a free gift card as a thank you.
CarbonNeutralIndiana.org/book-feedback

ONE

Electricity

"My brain is only a receiver. In the Universe
there is a core from which we obtain
knowledge, strength and inspiration. I
have not penetrated into the secrets
of this core, but I know that it exists."

— *Nikola Tesla*

OVERVIEW

Electricity includes activities like lighting, heating and cooling buildings, powering computers, and running myriad types of motors. Electricity generation produces 25% of human-made emissions globally. These emissions may increase in the near future, for at least two reasons. More of the economy (like transportation) will become electric. And, we still need to help 770 million people access electricity globally.

Project Drawdown identifies three categories for solutions in this sector. First, enhancing efficiency. This means reducing demand for electricity by making buildings and industry more efficient. Second, shifting from fossil fuels to solar, wind, geothermal, hydro, and nuclear power. Finally, improving the electricity system with flexible grids, more efficient transmission methods, and more storage.

Contrary to what some believe, Indiana has a track record of innovating in this field. The first electric streetlights in the nation were switched on in 1880 in the City of Wabash. In 2012, Ball State University installed the largest geothermal system of its kind in the world, saving $4 million annually. And soon, the largest solar farm in the United States will be in Knox, Indiana.

There's a lot to look forward to. Indiana could power 500,000 homes with untapped hydroelectric power. Mitch Daniels announced that Purdue could be the first university powered by small modular nuclear reactors (SMRs). And school districts are now able to apply for their share of $5 billion that Congress authorized in 2022 for electric school buses and charging infrastructure, through the Clean School Bus Program.

DRAWDOWN SOLUTIONS	Potential Reduction (Gt CO_2e)
Onshore wind turbines	97.5
Utility-scale solar photovoltaics	80.7
Distributed solar photovoltaics	48.3

Concentrated solar power	21.3
LED lighting	16.8
District heating	8.1
Geothermal power	8.0
Biomass power	3.0
Nuclear power	3.0
Small hydropower	2.5
Water distribution efficiency	0.8
Grid flexibility, microgrids, distributed energy storage	These solutions enable the others.

Saving $30,000 with Residential Solar

"I love thunderstorms. When the thunder struck, my mom told us to be quiet because God was working. We respected electricity."

Faye Moore grew up in Brooklyn, New York. She lived on the first floor of a brownstone with her cousins on the second and third floors. When she wasn't watching lightning, she was playing handball with the other kids. She moved to Indiana and settled in Michigan City, serving with the Indiana Department of Corrections for a few decades before retiring recently.

"I first heard about solar energy at an NAACP conference in 2011," Faye said. "But coal ash caught my attention." This toxic sludge produced by coal power plants contains heavy metals that can cause heart disease, respiratory illnesses, and stroke. Indiana has more coal ash ponds and landfills than any other state, and most are unlined and near major waterways.

The nonprofit Solar United Neighbors helped Faye determine eligibility and financing. She jumped at the chance to use clean energy. The $2,000 tax credit and saving $30,000 on her energy bill over 25 years were icing on the cake. "In Michigan City a lot of people have asthma," Faye said. "I feel better about using clean energy, and I'm encouraging friends and family to go solar too."

RESIDENTIAL SOLAR

Can I Do This?

COSTS

Money: the average 6 kilowatt solar system costs $15,300 in Indiana, and Faye's financing costs $130/mo. If installed in 2023, you'll receive a federal tax credit of 22% of the total cost. Roof space: the average system requires up to 345 square feet.

BENEFITS

Reduce CO_2: average solar system produces 7,800 kilowatts annually, eliminating 125 tons of CO_2 over 25 years. Equivalent to taking one car off the road. Cleaner air: Indiana leads the nation in toxic pollution emitted per square mile, according to the EPA's 2019 Toxic Release Inventory. Indiana also ranks ninth in cancer deaths. Cleaner water. Produce less coal ash: U.S. power plants produce enough coal ash annually to fill 1.3 million railroad cars stretching from New York City to San Francisco four times.

CHALLENGES

A south-facing roof is ideal. Trees might block sunlight. New roof: solar panels last about 25 years, so it's best to install them on a new roof. In Indiana, rooftop solar will not receive retail rate credit for any extra power that is contributed to the grid.

PROCESS	Attend a "Solar 101" class hosted by Solar United Neighbors (`SolarUnitedNeighbors.org`). Schedule a call to determine your eligibility. Review financing options.
ADVICE	Invest in your home's energy efficiency first (e.g. better insulation and windows, LED lights, tankless water heater, Energy Star appliances, fireplace insert, etc.).

City Finances Energy-Efficient Buildings

How could $220 billion improve your town? This amount of money is managed nationwide by Community Development Financial Institutions. CDFIs traditionally help large cities finance community projects. Smaller Indiana towns couldn't access their services — until now. Bloomington has become the first "CDFI Friendly" city in the nation. South Bend soon followed. Will your town be next?

Lauren Clemens is Bloomington's Assistant Director of Sustainability. She noticed a problem: local nonprofits wanted their buildings to be more energy efficient, but they often lacked the money to make those improvements. So when Bloomington received money from the federal American Rescue Plan, Lauren and her colleagues got creative.

First they paid for facility energy audits, $3,000 each. A technician analyzed how each building was using, and wasting, energy. The City then offered grants up to $10,000 to improve these buildings based on what the audits found.

The library switched to LED lighting. A daycare center upgraded to an efficient air conditioner. Other nonprofits weatherized their buildings or installed occupancy sensors to turn off lights when no one is around.

But energy efficiency is just the first step. The next is financing solar installations. And that's where CDFI Friendly Bloomington comes in. It helps connect community projects, like solar installs, to CDFIs around the nation that can finance them. This CDFI Friendly model pioneered in Bloomington is so promising it is being replicated in small towns around the country by CDFI Friendly America.

"I started working at the City because I believe in public service," Lauren said. "These nonprofits are operating on a tiny margin, doing a million things, trying to solve a problem. We're working together to make that happen."

CDFI FINANCING

Can I Do This?

COSTS

Free for the nonprofit. The City pays $3,000 per energy audit and $2,500–$10,000 for efficiency upgrades. Part of Bloomington's income tax goes to climate action. Lauren spent 50% of her full-time job for six months to start the project. Now it's 20% to maintain it. CDFI Bloomington has two full-time staff.

BENEFITS

Organizations save 25% on utility costs, according to the U.S. Department of Energy. In 2021, 11 Indiana organizations participated. Bloomington's successful model is being replicated in South Bend.

CHALLENGES

Finding experts who can do energy audits for small and medium buildings.

RESOURCES	Start with **CDFIFriendlyAmerica.com** and a webinar given by Lauren: **bit.ly/3bbgdkq**. See also: **OFN.org**
	CDFIFund.gov
	IFF.org
	CDFIFriendlyBtown.org
	CDFIFriendlySouthBend.org.

ADVICE	Start by understanding what your community needs. Don't assume anything — interview them to learn. Financing is often the main barrier to climate action, so study breakthrough tools like CDFIs. Don't worry if you don't have all the answers; figure it out as you go. Improve continuously. Narrow down grant opportunities to three to four specific ones you want to target.

How Schools Are Saving Millions of Dollars

"I sold pies for the basketball team as a kid. More than all the other sports teams combined — largely because I understood and cared deeply about my customers," Kelly Hipskind said.

"For example, I went to all of the grandmothers in the neighborhood and said, 'Think how much time you spend in the kitchen making pies. Instead, what if you bought enough for the whole year? You'd save a lot of time, and these pies are delicious!'"

Kelly is a born entrepreneur, and he's been helping schools since day one. It makes sense, because his parents were teachers in Northwest Indiana. His dad coached basketball at Portage, Hobart, and Greensburg. "I think this is pretty cool for basketball fans," Kelly said. "My dad was an assistant coach at DeMatha in DC when Mike Brey was also an assistant coach. Of course Mike went on to become the men's head coach at Notre Dame."

Kelly went on to co-found Sun FundED with his friend, Patrick Poer. They make it easy for schools to take advantage of solar energy, which cuts operating expenses and educates students about renewable energy.

"We wanted to find a way to have a measurable, positive impact on both schools and classrooms," Kelly said. "Something that would improve their budgets for years." So they assembled a board of advisors with people like Rafael Sanchez, former CEO of Indianapolis Power & Light. They spent time designing special financing called "Solar-as-a-Service," so schools don't pay money up front.

So far, it's working. Sun FundED has helped schools like Taylor University, Indiana Wesleyan University, and Franklin County Community School Corporation. Their current clients forecast savings of $75–$125 million. Sun FundED just announced a partnership with Indianapolis Public Schools, which will be the largest solar energy project by an educational institution in the state, and it's projected to save the school system $45 million over the next 30 years. They also developed an educational module for classrooms called SAMI™, in which students can review energy data from real world solar systems.

"We've had two main challenges. The first is that some people think solar is too good to be true. We can solve that with education. The other challenge is Indiana's regulatory environment, specifically net-metering. Hopefully in the next year or two, the State will get its ducks in a row. If just 20% of the public schools in Indiana adopt this Solar-as-a-Service model, they'll save $1 billion!"

EDUCATIONAL SOLAR
Can I Do This?

COSTS

Relative to current expenses: None. Schools do not pay for their solar systems up front. They only pay for the electricity, now cheaper, once the system is turned on.

BENEFITS

10–20% reduction in electricity costs. Better cash flow. No need to float a bond. It's not debt on the books because it's a service model. No need to manage projects long term: Solar-as-a-Service includes maintenance, insurance, warranties.

CHALLENGES

Lack of net metering in Indiana. Net metering means energy producers (like solar panel owners) are credited at the retail rate for the energy they contribute to the grid.

ADVICE

Believe in yourself. Do more than serve your customers, try to love them. You have a fiduciary duty to them. Innovation never starts at the top. It comes from an individual, like a tinkerer in a garage. When innovating, be patient. You won't get to scale in your first year.

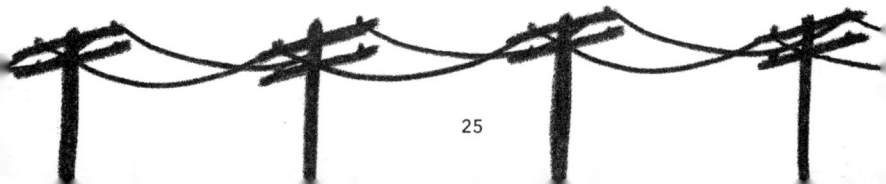

More Success Stories

Researchers at Oak Ridge National Laboratory found that Indiana has 791 megawatts (MW) of untapped hydroelectric power, **enough to power 500,000 homes.**

Research by Dr. Michael Wilcox and others at Purdue found that counties received more property tax revenue after installing wind turbines. Benton County received **an additional $492 per citizen per year.**

Carmel is the first city in the country to pilot Indiana-made hydrogen technology in its fleet. It's developed by AlGalCo, supplements existing engines, and **improves gas mileage 15–20%.**

Doral Renewable Energy Group will build a 13,000 acre solar farm in Knox, Indiana. This will be the **largest solar farm in the country,** enough to power 200,000 homes.

Purdue and Duke Energy are evaluating the feasibility of using small modular nuclear reactors (SMRs) to power the campus. Purdue would be the **first university in the country** to use this technology.

Notre Dame installed a small hydro power system for $27.1 million. It generates 2.5 MW of electricity, or about **7% of the university's needs.**

The Indianapolis International Airport built **the largest airport-based solar field in the world** in 2014.

Fort Wayne-based WaterFurnace is **a leading manufacturer** of geothermal and water source heat pumps.

The Indiana NAACP installed a solar system for the St. James Community Recreation and Education Center in Evansville. This **cut their energy costs by 40%.**

There are more than 610 uncapped, abandoned natural gas wells in Indiana, each of which leaks on average 6.75 tons of CO_2e annually. Indiana is eligible **to receive $39 million** from the Federal Orphaned Well Program to cap these wells.

Conservatives for a Clean Energy Future named **three Indiana elected officials 2021 Clean Energy Champions**: Sharon Negele (State Representative), Terry Smith (Shelby County Councilman), and Lloyd Winnecke (Evansville Mayor).

In 2021, Audubon Great Lakes released results of a statewide poll of Hoosiers about renewable energy. **Nearly 74% support expanding renewable energy sources.**

Directory of Organizations

Solar United Neighbors can help you install a solar system on your home or industrial building. Participate in bulk purchase programs called solar co-ops. Use their Solar Help Desk for free technical assistance. Schedule a free consultation at `SolarUnited Neighbors.org/indiana`

Solarize Indiana educates people about solar in Columbus, Bloomington, and Northern Indiana. `SolarizeIndiana.org`

Sun FundED is a solar project developer that only works with schools. School administrators can schedule a free consultation call to see if their school qualifies. Sun FundED also offers a solar energy module for STEM education. `SunFundED.com`

Electric School Bus Initiative is a newly launched program by World Resources Institute to help school districts invest in electric school buses. `WRI.org/initiatives/ electric-school-bus- initiative`

Directory continues on next page.

Citizens Action Coalition
is Indiana's oldest and largest consumer and environmental advocacy organization. Learn about bills at the state legislature. `CitAct.org`

Indiana Conservative Alliance for Energy
hosts a podcast and public events to educate Hoosiers about renewable energy. Running for office? See their polling data.
`IndianaConservative AllianceForEnergy.com`

International Ground Source Heat Pump Association
is the main hub for education in the geothermal industry. `IGSHPA.org`. See also the Geothermal Exchange Organization at `GeoExchange.org`

Indiana Geothermal
might be the largest geothermal installer in the state — over 6,000 systems in 25 years.
`IndianaGeothermal.com`

Indiana Clean Energy News
is a daily email about Indiana and the Midwest. Contact
`Jennifer@MassAvePR.com`

Indiana Solar for All helps Hoosiers with less than 80% of the area median income receive discounted residential solar systems. Participants pay it forward by helping others install solar systems. `INSFA.org`

Energy Systems Network
fosters cross-industry collaboration to improve Indiana's energy ecosystem, including generation, transmission, and the built environment. Projects so far include Hoosier Heavy Hybrid, Project Plug-IN, MicroGreen, and the Battery Innovation Center.
`EnergySystemsNetwork.com`

The Richard G. Lugar Center for Renewable Energy
researches renewable energy solutions such as solar energy, electric and hybrid vehicles, and waste-to-energy technologies. Currently 44 researchers participate. Learn more about their findings at `LugarEnergyCenter.org`

Legislation

2022 **HEA 1196 Homeowners associations and solar power.** Describes how people who live in an HOA and want to install solar can petition others in their HOA.

2022 **SB 271 Small modular nuclear reactors**. Requires the Indiana Utility Regulatory Commission and the Indiana Department of Environmental Management to outline the rules governing the construction, purchase, and leasing of small modular reactors, a technology used by the U.S. Navy for the past several decades.

2022 **SEA 251 Regulation of radioactive material.** Enters Indiana into a nuclear regulatory agreement with the U.S. Nuclear Regulatory Commission.

2022 **SEA 147 Underground pumped storage hydropower**. Energy storage at abandoned coal mines and quarries. Qualifies this technology as "clean energy resources" for the Indiana voluntary clean energy portfolio standard program.

2022 **SEA 411 Commercial solar and wind energy.** Establishes guidelines for siting renewable energy projects. Voluntary. Seeks to remove one bottleneck to expanding solar and wind in Indiana.

2021 **HEA 1191 Energy matters.** Prevents cities from prioritizing fuel sources. Prevents municipalities from banning new gas infrastructure during construction.

2021 **HEA 1220 21st Century Energy Policy Development Task Force** 15 members to review the state's energy policy. Will focus to balance energy reliability, resilience, stability, affordability, and the environment. Task force will submit a final report no later than Dec. 1, 2022.

Legislation continues on next page.

2017 **SEA 309 Distributed generation.** Ends net metering for solar energy. Instead of crediting energy producers, like households, with the retail value of electricity, they are credited at 25% above the wholesale price.

2016 **HB 1246** and **SB 308 Two changes to Classified Forest and Wildlands Program.** Enrolled land is now assessed at $13.29/acre and will be updated annually by the percentage change in the Consumer Price Index for All Urban Consumers.

2011 **SEA 251 Indiana's Clean Energy Portfolio Standard.** Voluntary. Sets a goal of 10% clean energy by 2025.

TWO

Food, Agriculture & Land Use

"Scientists in China [developed] a novel technology that turns CO_2 into starch in a highly efficient manner … Starch is an essential material for everything from bread-baking to paper-making … The entire process involves only 11 core reactions, and produces starch from CO_2 with 8.5 times the efficiency of corn …

The team believes the breakthrough offers a new scientific basis for new technologies that manufacture industrial quantities of starch from CO_2. Not only could this save on land and water, but it could also go a long way to shoring up food security and reduce the use of environmentally damaging pesticides and fertilizers."

— *Nick Lavars*, New Atlas, *September 2021*

OVERVIEW

Food, agriculture, and land use includes activities like growing food and producing fiber and timber. This sector produces 24% of human-made emissions globally, and it'll be increasingly important as both population and consumption increase.

Project Drawdown groups solutions in this sector into three categories. First, addressing food waste and diets. This means eating more plant-rich meals and reducing food waste. Second, protecting ecosystems. One indirect way to do this is to increase farm productivity, which reduces pressure on wild areas. Finally, shifting farming practices. Regenerative farming reduces emissions from manure and fertilizers, captures carbon in the soil, and improves soil health.

Indiana is ahead of the game. Why? Purdue University's research contributed to tripling total U.S. agricultural output between 1948 and 2015. This occurred even as labor requirements decreased by 75% and land requirements decreased by 24%. So not only does Indiana help feed the world, we're helping to reduce carbon emissions by producing that food more efficiently.

We have more reasons to be proud. More acres of cover crops are planted in Indiana than in any other state. And our timber industry is the nation's top producer of certain products, like office furniture. The carbon in wooden products is kept out of the atmosphere for decades, if not centuries. In fact, one of Drawdown's climate solutions involves treating wood so that it's strong enough to be used in skyscrapers. This can reduce global emissions by 14–31%. Indiana already captures carbon by growing forests. Now we can store it for longer and longer periods with new products.

DRAWDOWN SOLUTIONS	Potential Reduction (Gt CO_2e)
Reduced food waste	96.2
Plant-rich diets	78.3
Improved cattle feed	9.7

Nutrient management	7.2
Improved manure management	4.7
Farm irrigation efficiency	1.6
Improved aquaculture	0.6

School Rescues Wasted Food

"A $10,000 industrial refrigerator? We can't afford that!"

Sitting in a meeting are the superintendent of Hamilton Heights School Corporation, the Director of Food Services, the founder of K12 Food Rescue John Williamson, and Audra Shock, a volunteer at a local food pantry.

"Think of all of the great food students throw away," John said. "Unopened boxes of milk. Untouched carrots and apples. Perfectly good oranges. Instead of wasting, it we can collect it in coolers and then give it to a food pantry."

There was only one catch. The town pantry didn't have a refrigerator to keep perishable items. They could only store cans and dried goods.

But the next day, Audra's father got a phone call. It was the local pharmacy. "We're closing for good — know anyone who wants a large refrigerator?"

"Part of me can't believe it," Audra said. "But a lot of times, things just work out in ways you don't expect."

And now, 2,300 students save untouched food. 300,000 items, enough to feed 40 families three meals a day for a year.

Years later, Audra moved to Noblesville and helped that school district join K12 Food Rescue too. Students even organized a club, collected the food, counted it, and calculated its environmental impact. Her daughter made a documentary about it.

"My parents taught me an important lesson," Audra said. "Sometimes you need help, and sometimes you help others. I was a single mother, but I was blessed to live near my parents. I'm happy to help."

Can I Do This?

COSTS

2–3 hours to educate the school and cafeteria leadership. Someone to drive to a pantry once a week. $200 for a 2.5 ft cooler for each lunch room. Signage. Refrigerator.

BENEFITS

Food pantry receives $3–$5K of free milk, carrots, apples, etc. annually. A school with 1,000 students rescuing food would reduce about 8.1 tons CO_2e annually, similar to taking two cars off the road. Improved relationships. Enlightened, active students.

PROCESS

Begin the journey at FoodRescue.net

RESOURCES

Learn more at Leanpath.com and ReFED.org

Annual Event Celebrates Plant-Rich Lifestyle

100 vendors serving every food imaginable. Mouth watering Chicago-style deep dish pizza. Homemade pasta. Indian, Vietnamese, Turkish cuisine… and fresh sushi! Or maybe you just want a snack. Popcorn, cookies, ice cream, chocolate, truffles, toffee, caramels. And then there are the drinks. Juice, chai, kombucha, the aromatic coffee you know will take you to another level. Welcome to Indy VegFest!

In 1993, Katelin Rupp read the book *Diet for a New America*, and decided to be a vegan. In 2017, she co-founded Indy VegFest — an annual, free festival in Indianapolis celebrating plant-rich lifestyles.

The event hosts local and national speakers, documentary screenings, and community nonprofits. But the audience favorite is the astounding variety of vegetarian and vegan food vendors.

"[Hoosiers] love trying new kinds of food," Katelin observed. Throughout it all, she and her team try to be as non-judgmental as possible. "Food is very personal for people. It's critical that we're welcoming and have open arms."

The result? In just a few years, they've grown to over 5,000 attendees.

But organizing this festival isn't her day job … yet. She's the Director of Program Evaluation at the Indiana State Department of Health, overseeing evaluation for the Tobacco Prevention and Cessation Commission and the Indiana Tobacco Control Strategic Plan.

Indy VegFest took a two-year break because of the pandemic, but it'll be back in 2023. Katelin's advice? "Let's not judge anyone for their eating and living lifestyles. Respect them, and welcome them to try healthier options where they'll feel better, more alive, with greater energy."

PLANT-RICH FOOD EVENT

Can I Do This?

COSTS	5–10 hours/week for six months to organize and promote a large event. Space to host event. Advertising.
BENEFITS	Bringing people together. Encouraging climate-positive behavior. Supporting local food entrepreneurs. Education.
CHALLENGES	Food is personal, an identity issue. Take care to be welcoming and encouraging.

ADVICE Attract food vendors. Market to everyone, not just vegetarians/vegans. Emphasize health benefits. Promote easy changes, like #MeatlessMonday. Advertise with inclusivity in mind. Partner with nonprofits so they can exhibit on-site and promote to their networks. Watch the documentary *Forks Over Knives*.

More Success Stories

Nonprofit Cultivate Food Rescue partners with Notre Dame to rescue food from football games. Untouched food is frozen and **distributed to those who need it.**

Leanpath creates **food waste prevention technology**, used by Notre Dame and Reid Health, a hospital in central Indiana.

Notre Dame uses the Grind2Energy system to process 99% of nonconsumable food waste. **2,000 pounds per day** is ground into energy-rich slurry, processed by a methane digester, and turned into clean energy.

The Kroger Co. Foundation, the U.S. Environmental Protection Agency, Earth Charter Indiana, and K12 Food Rescue created the Food Waste Warriors project in Indianapolis. **Six schools participate.**

University of Indianapolis participates in Food Recovery Network, a national program. **They deliver food to two shelters,** Wheeler Mission and Partners in Housing.

Feeding cows certain all-natural foods like garlic, citrus, and red algae from Asia, **can reduce methane emissions by 30%.**

Dr. Robert Kramer, a physics professor at Purdue Northwest, invented technology that creates **hydrogen from food waste.**

In 2023, the official fuel of the Indianapolis 500 will be **100% renewable race fuel** made from food waste, like sugar cane.

Directory of Organizations

FOOD WASTE & DIET

Indy VegFest hosts an annual event to educate the public about the benefits of a plant-rich lifestyle. They also host educational activities like free plant-based cooking classes throughout the year. **IndyVegFest.org**. Also see **BloomingVeg.org**

K12 Food Rescue is a program you can implement at your local school to teach kids about food waste and help them collect and donate untouched, unused food to a food pantry. **FoodRescue.net**

Cultivate Food Rescue in northern Indiana partners with supermarkets, restaurants, manufacturers, and caterers to rescue food and donate it to those in need. **CultivateCulinary.com**

ReFED is a national organization that reduces food waste. Their Insights Engine is a database of statistics, local partners, and solutions. The Catalytic Grant Fund finances food waste start-ups. Their Food Recovery Accelerator helps nonprofits working on food rescue innovations. **ReFED.org**

Local Harvest is a directory of local, community-supported agriculture (CSAs) throughout the country. **LocalHarvest.org**

The Food Architect creates and delivers vegan meals throughout central Indiana. **TheFoodArchitectIndy.com**. Also, **BlackLeafVegan.com**, a food truck selling vegan meals in Indianapolis.

Directory continues on next page.

Indiana Association of Soil and Water Conservation Districts
helps farmers shift to regenerative farming practices that
protect and sink carbon into soil. **Wordpress.IASWCD.org**

Conservation Cropping Systems Initiative of Indiana promotes
soil health to Indiana farmers via educational curriculum, in-per-
son training, and a monthly podcast. They also help companies
meet their agriculture-related sustainability goals. **CCSIN.org**

Indiana Agriculture Nutrient Alliance Inc. educates
farmers in nutrient management, soil health, and water quality.
INAgNutrients.org

Legislation

PENDING **Growing Climate Solutions Act.** Federal legislation
introduced by Indiana Senator Mike Braun.
Directs the Department of Agriculture to create a
certification process for vendors who help farmers
sequester carbon through carbon markets.

2021 **SEA 389 Wetlands.** Removes state protections
of half of Indiana's wetlands. Applies to more
than 40,000 acres, 15% of what remains. Creates
a 13-member taskforce to study and reform wetland
protections, including studying CO_2 storage benefits.

THREE

Industry

"It's okay to use the current infrastructure to build the world of tomorrow. What else could you do? Henry Ford rode a horse. Thomas Edison used candlelight."

— *Unknown*

OVERVIEW

Industry makes things. It includes every step of the process, from mining raw materials, to manufacturing products, to disposing or reusing those products. Industry makes up 21% of human-made emissions globally.

Project Drawdown identifies four categories of solutions in this sector. First, improving materials like plastic, metal, and cement – or inventing alternatives. Cement production alone produces 8% of global emissions. Second, reimagining and reusing 'waste' (i.e. creating the "circular economy"). Third, better management and disposal of potent greenhouse gases used in refrigerators and air conditioners. And lastly, making all industrial processes more energy efficient.

In Indiana, manufacturing is 12 times bigger than agriculture, producing 26.4% of the state's gross domestic product in 2009. We can be proud of this history. Indiana-based Eli Lilly was the first company to mass-produce penicillin, which saved 200 million lives. Electric motors consume 40% of global electricity. Regal-Rexnord, another Indiana company, invented the electronically commutated motor, which reduces energy consumption by 80%. Indiana also produces more steel than any other state, and is the sixth largest exporter of automobiles in the country. And thanks to Greg Ballard, former Mayor of Indianapolis, Hoosiers also lead the way encouraging the next generation of manufacturing innovation, hosting the largest robotics state championship in the country with over 200 K-12 teams.

Companies in Indiana are already positioning themselves to win in the decarbonized economy. The Heritage Group owns the largest lithium battery recycler in North America. SDI Biocarbon Solutions will reduce emissions from steelmaking by 20–25%. Wabash Valley Resources is retrofitting an old coal gasification plant to produce hydrogen that will power factories and transportation.

Refrigerant management	57.8
Alternative refrigerants	47.0
Alternative cement	12.0
Methane digesters	8.0
Recycling	5.3
Composting	2.6
Waste-to-energy	2.5
Bioplastics	2.4
Recycled paper	1.5
Landfill methane capture	0.3

INDUSTRY

Turning Sewage and Grease into Energy

"Sewage? I never planned to work on this," Doug Fasick said. "But I enjoy it. It's exciting actually."

Doug and his family are perfect examples of how land-grant universities improve society. Doug's father left the family farm to study horticultural engineering at Purdue, and earned four patents. Doug later studied mechanical engineering at the Fort Wayne campus.

Today, Doug is Senior Programs Manager for Fort Wayne City Utilities. The process of removing pollutants from residential and industrial water and returning it to waterways accounts for 3% of global emissions. That's right, the treatment of wastewater has the emissions equivalent of air travel. A lot of electricity is used to move around 100 million gallons of water a day in Fort Wayne, enough to fill a 17-story building the size of a football field. Not to mention the biological waste produces methane, a potent greenhouse gas.

In 2013, Mayor Tom Henry and Utilities Director Kumar Menon looked for ways to reduce these emissions. Fort Wayne ended up building two methane digesters, and Doug upgraded the city's wastewater treatment facility to incorporate them. These 400 kilowatt digesters capture methane from waste, and burn it to produce electricity. This reduces emissions from the plant, while cutting its electricity use by 30%. It also saved them $1.2 million over two years.

Digesters cost a lot to build, something Doug thinks communities can solve by collaborating regionally. What if other communities sent their organic waste to existing digesters in West Lafayette, Evansville, and Indianapolis?

Fort Wayne found this to be profitable. They import three truckloads of waste a day from the Nestlé plant in Anderson, and they're exploring importing Huntington's waste as well. Fort Wayne even started the City Utilities Grease Cooperative to collect grease from 1,500 restaurants.

"We're always looking to improve efficiency," Doug said. "We do energy audits annually, and we've already identified 70 other ways we can reduce carbon emissions."

METHANE DIGESTER

Can I Do This?

COSTS	Roughly $6,000 per kilowatt up front to build a digester and $53 per kilowatt in annual maintenance.
BENEFITS	Reduce electricity bill by 30%. Increase resiliency by generating some electricity onsite.
CHALLENGES	The Indiana Department of Environmental Management, electric utilities, and municipalities need to collaborate more to reduce electricity costs and provide end consumers with the clean energy they are demanding.

RESOURCES
The ENVISION tool by the Institute For Sustainable Infrastructure. Also, Dana Kirk's research at Michigan State University.

ADVICE
Companies like NOVI Energy LLC can help your city do feasibility studies. Research renewable natural gas incentives. Take it slow and learn one step at a time.

Recycling Urban Trees Into Art

If a tree falls in the city, does anyone hear it? Of course they do … it's in the city! The real question is: will it be recycled into something beautiful?

Indiana artist Brian Presnell embodied the circular economy before it was a thing. His grandmother was a real-life Rosie the Riveter, making ammunition during World War II. "Recycling metal was a life or death issue to defeat the Germans," Brian said. "Even Abbott and Costello joked about how valuable rubber was."

Brian grew up in a single-parent household on the westside of Indianapolis. He earned money washing limos, but he loved to draw. "Why don't you apply to Herron School of Art + Design?" said Larry Hurt, his art teacher at Ben Davis High School. His friend's father, Richard Moran, helped him apply for financial aid.

"These two men saved my life," Brian said. He learned to design interior spaces, specializing in art exhibits. "I've hung million-dollar Warhol paintings," Brian said, referring to one of his Hoosier art collector clients. And he started designing furniture. "Most of the people who read this book have probably sat at a wooden dining table I've made. They're at locally owned restaurants throughout Indiana, like Bluebeard in Indianapolis."

In 2000, the Indianapolis Museum of Art (now Newfields) cut down trees on their property. Brian asked if he could recycle the logs. "Sure, why not," the museum official said. He brought his Wood-Mizer portable sawmill and rescued trees from the woodchipper. Years later, in 2016, he started Indy Urban Hardwood Co. and began making art from the reclaimed wood. He creates custom furniture for residential and commercial clients: everything from tables, bars, and counters for restaurants to shelving and full interior installs for homes and art collectors.

"By this point, I've rescued at least half a million board feet from the mulch pile," Brian said. "That carbon is trapped in gorgeous products families will enjoy for hundreds of years. One woman had a huge ash tree. Her children loved playing on its tree swing, but the tree died from emerald ash borer. They were devastated. So I made it into furniture for them. I hope to show Hoosiers how beautiful our trees are. We can give them a second life."

RECLAIMED WOOD FURNISHINGS
Can I Do This?

COSTS
Complimentary email or phone consultation for custom work. Side and coffee tables range from $150–$1,600. Custom walnut shelves start at $325.

BENEFITS
Most wood from Indiana contains about 4.5 pounds of CO_2 per board foot. The half a million board feet Brian has rescued would be roughly 1,125 tons of CO_2. This is equivalent to installing solar on eight homes.

RESOURCES

Contact Brian at IndyUrbanHardwood.com.
See also Harmony Hardwoods in Bloomington
at HarmonyHardwoods.shop, and Big Tooth Co. in
Fort Wayne at BigToothCo.com.

More Success Stories

The world's first carbon-neutral eggs will be produced
in North Manchester, IN by MPS Egg Farms.

Indiana's Steel Dynamics created a joint venture called
SDI Biocarbon Solutions. They plan to **reduce carbon
emissions from steel production by 20–25%.**

Dun Agro Hemp Group, Inc. is building a hemp
factory in Indiana. They pioneered **hempcrete,
an alternative to high-emissions traditional
cement.** See also Facebook.com/PurdueHemp.

Purdue researcher Mirian Velay-Lizancos found that
adding titanium dioxide to cement can **double its
natural ability to sequester carbon dioxide.**

Kinetrex Energy will capture methane from three landfills (in
Danville, Wyatt, and Monticello) to create renewable natural gas.
This will generate enough gas for **56,000 households annually.**

Sortera Alloys is opening a manufacturing facility
in Fort Wayne that **uses artificial intelligence
to sort scrap metal for new products.**

The Northeast Indiana Solid Waste Management District
funded a successful pilot program by Brightmark in Ashley,
IN. Every year, Brightmark will **repurpose 1.2 million tons
of plastic** types 1 through 7, turning them into fuel and wax.

INDUSTRY

Directory of Organizations

Circular Indiana
advocates for systems which reuse materials to create a circular economy. They host an annual Innovation Summit and an online Master Recycler Program. **CircularIndiana.org**

Composting services
pick up food waste and turn it into products like soil. Is there is a service near you?

Earth Mama Compost, Green With Indy, Indy Go Green in Indianapolis, **RE317** in Hamilton County, **EarthKeepers** in Bloomington, **Dirt Wayne** and **Ground Down** in Fort Wayne, **Wabash ReThinks** in Terre Haute, and **Go Greener Commission** in West Lafayette.

Association of Indiana Solid Waste Management Districts
is an advisory group that oversees the rules and legislation for recycling, reducing, and reusing in Indiana. Offers educational events for members. **AISWMD.org**

RecycleForce
employs formerly incarcerated people to recycle electronics. Offers an Indianapolis drop off location for old electronic devices. **RecycleForce.org**

Recycling Market Development Program
hosts quarterly meetings to discuss issues, share resources, and find solutions to current challenges facing recyclers and Indiana's recycling industry. They also award grants from $50,000–$500,000. **bit.ly/3baYWre**

EPA GreenChill Program helps retailers reduce leakage of refrigerants for free. These chemicals can have 7,000 times the impact of carbon dioxide. **EPA.gov/greenchill**

North American Sustainable Refrigeration Council helps stakeholders in the supermarket industry learn about and advocate for climate-friendly natural refrigerants with ultra-low global warming potential. **NASRC.org**

AES Appliance Recycling Program accepts old fridges and freezers, and pays residents $50 per appliance to properly dispose of them. They will also accept air conditioners and dehumidifiers for a fee. **866-472-9381**

Midwest Cogeneration Association helps employees educate organizations about combined heat and power: technology that harnesses the heat from electricity generation. `Cogeneration.org`

Clean Energy Buyers Alliance teaches industry actors about the clean energy market. `CEBuyers.org`

Indiana University IoT Energy Efficiency Lab helps manufacturers save money by using less energy. Their smart meters provide a "sleep mode" for factories. They've already helped save $200 million. Contact Professor Amrou Awaysheh at `Awaysheh@IU.edu`

Legislation

2018 **Definition of Solid Waste.** A specific definition by the EPA which 14 states have fully adopted. Indiana has not. Pertains to recycling of hazardous materials. Advocated for by the Indiana Manufacturers Association.

2022 **HEA 1226 Wetlands.** Updates Indiana's solid waste law to be consistent with the federal government's. Creates the Central Indiana Waste Diversion Pilot Program, including $4 million for recycling infrastructure.

2022 **HEA 1226 American Innovation and Manufacturing (AIM) Act.** Directs EPA to phase down the production and use of refrigerant gases by 85% over 15 years.

Transportation & Buildings

"You take the mortar, block, and glass
And you forget the speech
that moved the stone"

— *Ben Folds, "Philosophy"*

OVERVIEW

Transportation & buildings include moving people and things via planes, trains, automobiles, and boats, as well as constructing and operating buildings. This sector produces 20% of human-made emissions globally.

Project Drawdown groups solutions in this sector into four categories. First, alternative transportation which includes public transit, more compact cities, and even remote working. Next, we need to enhance efficiency. For buildings, we can improve insulation and use next generation HVAC technology. We also need to electrify both transportation and buildings with technologies like electric vehicles, heat pumps, electric ranges, and induction cooktops. Finally, refrigerants must be addressed. These are used in air conditioners and refrigerators, but they can trap 7,000 times more heat in the atmosphere than carbon dioxide. We need to reduce leakage, dispose of them properly, and replace them with better technologies.

As the "Crossroads of America," Indiana ranks transportation and logistics among our most important industries. The Indianapolis International Airport won Best Airport in North America for 10 years in a row. Our railroads transport 277 million tons of cargo per year. And FedEx selected Indianapolis for its second-largest facility.

Indiana researchers are already decarbonizing both transportation and buildings. Purdue scientists earned a Guinness World Record for the whitest paint in the world. When painted on the roof of a building, the paint reflects sunlight and can reduce energy use by 20%. Other Purdue researchers and the Indiana Department of Transportation (INDOT) are creating the nation's first stretch of highway that can charge electric vehicles (EVs) wirelessly.

TRANSPORTATION	Public transit	15.4
	Electric cars	13.7
	Efficient aviation	7.7
	Efficient trucks	7.1
	Hybrid cars	6.2
	Carpooling	5.9
	Bicycle infrastructure	3.6
	Walkable cities	3.4
BUILDINGS	Insulation	17.9
	High-performance glass	11.3
	Solar hot water	8.9
	Building automation systems	8.4
	Smart thermostats	7.1
	High-efficiency heat pumps	6.7

Ordinance Limits New Gas Stations

What does childhood leukemia have to do with gas stations? Benzene. Research suggests that this chemical in gasoline increases the risk of cancers, respiratory issues, and birth defects.

But professional wedding photographer Jackie Phillips didn't know that in 2020. After 10 years in the profession, she wondered what was next for her. That's when she saw it. A post on social media — a gas station was coming to West Clay.

At first she only worried about her home value, but her research soon led her to the connection between benzene and childhood cancer. She went to her homeowners association. They weren't helpful. One board member was the person trying to sell the land for the gas station. So she hosted an event in her backyard, created a website, and passed out fliers and yard signs.

Some city leaders were critics. She won them over with persistence and education. Others remained silent. So she continued growing an email list ... and political will. It wasn't easy. She worked, unpaid, for two years with her husband's support. Eventually Jackie rallied the community to pass a city ordinance: no new gas stations within 500 feet of a school or home. But the developer threatened to sue the City. So she raised $25,000 from the community, hired four attorneys, and pushed back successfully.

"It's satisfying," she said. "It felt like David vs. Goliath. I was in a professional funk, and this gave me a new purpose. Already three other cities have reached out for help. And I developed friendships with neighbors." The fewer gas stations we build, the faster we'll transition to mostly electric transportation.

LIMIT NEW GAS STATIONS
Can I Do This?

COSTS	Opportunity costs from two years of full-time, unpaid work totaling $150,000. $23,000 for legal costs. $2,000 for an industrial printer for fliers, yard signs, etc.
BENEFITS	Decreased cancer risks. Sense of accomplishment. Satisfaction when other cities reached out for help. Meaning. Aesthetics. Safety. 10% of crime happens at gas stations, including 63,000 violent crimes throughout the country every year. Less traffic. each gas pump brings 500–800 cars daily. Relationships. Got to know neighbors.

PROCESS	Research → Organize first meeting. → Create website, collect emails. → Email neighbors. → Create fliers, yard signs. → Conduct neighborhood survey. → Meet with and educate media. → Raise money. → Meet with attorneys. → Speak at City Council and committee meetings.
CHALLENGES	HOAs and city leaders were not supportive at first. Legal threats and costs. Finding an attorney interested in taking the case.
RESOURCES	CEDS.org, HECWeb.org, Research at Columbia and Johns Hopkins on cancer and respiratory issues.
ADVICE	Prepare to be vilified. Be patient. Engage city officials. Build relationships. People were persuaded by health issues, not climate.

Bringing Electric Transportation to Central Indiana

Why does Kevin Whited love the future? His father's tiny helicopter. It was little more than a pilot's seat and a rotor. Yet the Bensen Gyro-Copter climbed to 12,000 feet and traveled 100 miles. It captured Kevin's imagination. "People in the neighborhood always asked, 'What's up with your Dad?' He was an eccentric guy, and in 1989 he bought an electric car."

Decades later, Kevin is the Transportation Development Coordinator for the City of Carmel. He oversees plans for bicycle, pedestrian, and electric vehicle (EV) infrastructure.

One day in 2019, he got an email about National Drive Electric Week. Anyone can easily host this event in their city:

EV owners bring their vehicles to a parking lot, sit next to them, and answer questions. Some even take attendees on their first drive in an EV. Often, the best way to get people to switch is a simple test drive. "Why don't we host that event here?" he thought.

Kevin started by asked local nonprofits to promote the event. Then he bought a few ads in local newspapers. That first year, over 100 people attended. The pandemic forced them to take a break for two years, but at the second event, 250 attended, including 35 EV owners and a few local car dealerships.

"I like to look at what's new and innovative and see if it works for us," Kevin said. Anyone who's driven an EV knows that, like a helicopter, EVs fly. His father would be proud. Kevin is bringing the future of transportation to Central Indiana.

ELECTRIC VEHICLE EVENT
Can I Do This?

COSTS
40–50 hours. $1,000 for ads in local papers, graphic design, thank you cards.

BENEFITS
Health & energy. Cleaner air: car exhaust includes toxic chemicals like benzene, sulfur dioxide, and carbon monoxide. Also, electricity is usually produced far from homes. "Also happiness," Kevin said. "EVs are more fun to drive." Savings: fewer maintenance costs. Aesthetics: EVs are quieter.

PROCESS
Learn more from DriveElectricWeek.org. → Register to organize an event. → Find someone with a parking lot near a busy area. → Find community partners. → Create posters. → Invite auto dealers. → Have partners promote the event.

CHALLENGES	Canceled two years in a row because of the pandemic. Portions of the public may be unknowledgeable about EVs and therefore might be resistant to them. Resistance from some city councilors.
RESOURCES	FullyCharged.live website as inspiration. DriveElectricWeek.org. Also see HoosierEVA.org.
ADVICE	Plan in advance to secure a parking lot. Hold event during official Drive Electric Week for more support. Host during another event, like a farmers market. Invite a musician to play live.

Town Saves Money With White Roofs

Imagine a small town: the central square, the old buildings. You walk up to a building and run your fingers along its rough wall. It was built in 1905 (the year Las Vegas was founded). Think of the American history it's seen: that same year, Indiana sent Charles Fairbanks to the Whitehouse as Vice President. And the Wright Brothers kept their third plane aloft for 39 minutes.

The best part of Indiana might be our small towns. The heart of each one is its historic district. But these older buildings cost more to operate, and if their roofs aren't maintained properly, they'll be destroyed by rain. Cities will spend $250,000 on average to demolish the building while erasing part of the small-town culture. These buildings are meaningful, and once they're gone we can't get them back.

Enter Bryn Keplinger. He grew up in Huntington — population 17,000 — and remembers playing baseball at Gemmer Field. He attended Ball State, earned his masters in urban planning, and returned to Huntington. Today he's the city's Director of Community Development & Redevelopment.

The city participated in the Resilience Cohort, a project by Indiana University's Environmental Resilience Institute. "They helped us measure Huntington's carbon footprint," Bryn said. "Someone mentioned that white roofs reflect sunlight, reducing a building's energy needs and carbon emissions."

So he created Huntington's Commercial Facade & Roof Grant Program. If the owner of a historic building wants to replace their roof, the City will pitch in $5,000. The only catch is, the roof has to be white.

"Nobody even notices the roof. The buildings are too tall," Bryn said. "The downtown makes the city. Those buildings are worth caring about and saving. We're doing this for the next generation and taking our future into our own hands."

WHITE-ROOF PRESERVATION
Can I Do This?

COSTS

City grants $5,000 per roof, reducing the cost of the average $40,000 roof by 12%.

BENEFITS

Lowers energy costs 20% or more, reducing carbon emissions. Preserves historic buildings. Encourages building owners to invest in preventative maintenance by replacing their roof. Reduces city costs. No need to pay $250,000 to demolish decrepit buildings. Reduces heat in the downtown area.

PROCESS

Establish that saving downtown buildings matters and costs money to maintain and save. Speak with someone who's done a program like this. Find an example of your town demolishing a building. How much did it cost? Realize that a new roof would have been cheaper than demolishing the building. Sell the Mayor and City Council on the idea.

ADVICE

It's wise to preserve these buildings, and preventative maintenance is a good investment. Show how it saves everyone money. Rome wasn't built in a day. You're not going to win every battle. Take baby steps. They turn into strides.

More Success Stories

TRANSPORTATION

INDOT, Purdue, and Magment are creating the **first section of highway in the nation** that charges electric vehicles wirelessly.

The EPA's Clean School Bus Program is giving school districts **$500 million annually** for five years to shift to electric school buses.

Purdue Professor Issam Mudawar invented a new charging cable that can charge EVs in just five minutes, **4.6 times faster than the fastest Tesla supercharger.**

Motor EV provides an **electric vehicle subscription** service to central Indiana. Download the app, select plan and car, schedule charger installation, and start driving an electric vehicle.

Purdue engineer Chisom Emegoakor helped create Remora Carbon, a logistics startup company. Semi-truck drivers can use their technology to capture carbon and sell it at gas stations for industrial use. Pays for itself in two years. **Could reduce national emissions 6%.**

In August 2019 the Bargersville Police Department became **one of the first departments in the country to use the Tesla Model 3 as a squad car.** Since then they've added three more to the fleet.

BUILDINGS

Purdue scientists earned a Guinness Record for the **whitest paint in the world.** Painted on roofs, it can reflect sunlight and reduce energy use by 20%.

Indianapolis Public Schools was recognized by the U.S. Department of Energy for **reducing energy use by 26%.**

The Indianapolis Office of Sustainability created the Thriving Buildings program. Building owners **report their energy use publicly.**

The Cope Environmental Center in Centerville is the **first Living Building certified building in Indiana,** 29th in the world.

Notre Dame's Joyce Center has the **largest green roof in the state.** This vegetation-covered roof helps keep the building cool. Green roofs also exist at Children's Museum of Indianapolis, Ball Memorial Hospital, WFYI office, Orangutan Center at the Indianapolis Zoo, Eli Lilly, Schmidt Associates, and elsewhere.

Directory of Organizations

Central Indiana Regional Transportation Authority works to improve sustainable transportation in Indiana. Three programs help you travel safely and affordably: Commuter Connect, Workforce Connect, and County Connect. Start by calculating how much you spend on your commute: `bit.ly/3O6SDDL`. See also `Cirta.us`.

Bike Indianapolis improves bike infrastructure. They also host a cycling club. `BikeIndianapolis.org`

Hoosier Electric Vehicles Association hosts monthly meetings in Central Indiana for EV enthusiasts. `HoosierEVA.org`

Greater Indiana Clean Cities, Inc. helps organizations assess their fleets and develop alternative fuel programs. They also assist with research and grant writing. `GreaterIndiana.com`

Drive Clean Indiana helps schools reduce emissions by shifting to propane or electric buses. They offer training, grant funding, and project management. `DriveCleanIndiana.org`

Electric Vehicle Product Commission A 10-member group that evaluates the status and opportunities of the EV industry in Indiana. The commission will publish annual reports and operate through 2026.

American Institute of Architects can connect you to local architects who have signed the AIA 2030 net-zero commitment. `AIA.org` and `AIAIndiana.org`

ENERGY STAR certifies buildings when they are more energy efficient than 75% of similar buildings. `EnergyStar.gov`

American Society of Heating, Refrigerating and Air-Conditioning Engineers promotes the codes for energy standards and the design and construction of green buildings. `IndyASHRAE.org`

Directory continues on next page.

TRANSPORTATION & BUILDINGS

U.S. Green Building Council
maintains the LEED certification, ensuring buildings
are economical, efficient, and will operate sustainably.
Become a USGBC member to keep up to date with the
latest green building regulations and innovative practices. **USGBC.org** and `USGBC.org/chapters/usgbc-indiana`

Legislation

HEA 1221 Electric vehicles and electricity pricing.
2022 Creates the beginnings of a regulatory framework
for EV charging. Businesses like gas stations can
sell electricity but they must buy electricity from
utilities, rather than generate it from solar panels.

**HEA 1168 Electric vehicles and advanced
technology.** Creates the Electric Vehicle
2021 Product Commission with 10 members.

HEA 1236 Electric bicycles. Better defines e-bikes.
2019 Motorists are required to give three or more feet of
clearance when passing. Statewide education of motorists
about safe passing. Based on model legislation from People
for Bikes, Bicycle Products and Suppliers Association.

HEA 1649 Electric foot scooters. Establishes that
2019 scooters are to be treated as bicycles, not as motor
vehicles. Allows e-scooters to be parked on sidewalks.

HEA 1362 Peer to peer vehicle sharing.
2019 Authorizes P2P car sharing. Includes requirements
for companies, drivers, and vehicle owners.

FIVE

Carbon Sinks

"When you add up the impact on carbon sequestration and storage, forest protection and tropical and temperate forest restoration together are the most powerful solution available to address global warming."

— *Paul Hawken,* Drawdown: The Most Comprehensive Plan Ever Proposed to Reverse Global Warming

OVERVIEW

Carbon sinks take carbon out of the air and store it in a place where it can't cause global warming. They might be land sinks, storing it in soil and trees. Or engineered sinks, capturing it from exhaust and injecting it underground as a liquid, or turning it into solids like biochar and carbonate, or using it to create products like cement or sustainable jet fuel. Engineers around the world are researching both land and engineering sinks in order to pull existing emissions out of the air.

Project Drawdown hasn't assessed engineered sinks yet, but identifies four categories of land sinks. First, reducing food waste and shifting to plant-rich diets. This reduces pressure on natural ecosystems like forests. Second, protecting and restoring peatlands, grasslands, and forests. Third, shifting to regenerative farming practices like cover crops, no-till, and agroforestry. And finally, restoring farmlands that have been abandoned due to degradation.

Here's a success story: in 1920, just 6.2% of Indiana's land was forest, and we were losing 92,000 acres annually. A year later, the legislature reduced property taxes on forests. Now over 20% of Indiana is forest. Between 1998 and 2008, the state gained an average of 28,900 acres of forest annually. Today, our forests increase in volume 3.8 times faster than they are removed.

And there are many other reasons to be hopeful. Next in this chapter: a single Hoosier plants 80,000 trees. Storing carbon in soil is a major climate solution and makes food production more efficient and resilient. And new technologies might capture and store all of our emissions for tens of thousands of years.

DRAWDOWN SOLUTIONS	Potential Reduction (Gt CO_2e)
Tropical forest restoration	69.8
Silvopasture	34.4
Peatland protection and rewetting	34.0

Tree plantations on degraded lands	29.1
Temperate forest restoration	23.6
Perennial staple crops	23.4
Managed grazing	21.2
Tree intercropping	19.7
Regenerative annual cropping	18.4
Multistrata agroforestry	15.9
Conservation agriculture	11.4
Indigenous peoples' forest tenure	10.8
Forest protection	7.1
Perennial biomass production	5.5
Grassland protection	3.8
Biochar production	3.3

Man Plants 80,000 Trees Over 30 Years

"I'll be dead before those little sticks you're planting are grown trees," his father said. "Maybe," thought Will. "But planting trees is so rewarding. The earlier you start the more you have to appreciate as you age. Why not start today?"

Will Ditzler was five years old when he started caring for the planet. "We were traveling on a highway, and I saw so much trash along the road. It bothered me. I imagined a giant machine that would vacuum it all up."

He studied business at Indiana University, but an environmental biology class taught by Don Whitehead changed his life. "I majored in finance, but my heart was in ecology and wildlife." So Will joined an ecological restoration company and planted trees in his free time. "Two thousand trees a year adds up," Will said.

Eventually he became president of the company he joined, and helped grow it to 150 employees. Now Will is an executive coach, helping other companies grow. He's advised over 50 companies and nonprofits, including 1% for the Planet, an organization whose members contribute part of their revenue to environmental causes. He also serves on the board of The Nature Conservancy in Indiana.

Over the years, Will bought more land and planted more trees. He's been at it for 30 years. His father is still alive and can see those first trees that are now 50-foot tall oaks.

"This forest used to be just a worn-out farm, suffering from 100 years of conventional farming practices," Will said. "It was a monoculture of corn and beans, a biological desert. Now it's full of life."

TREE PLANTING
Can I Do This?

COSTS

Land: Will's average cost is $2,000 per acre. Low-quality land is $5,000–$6,000 per acre. Labor: a person can plant 200 seedlings per day by hand. Subsidized seedlings cost $0.50–$1.00 each. Weed control for 2–3 years.

BENEFITS

A grown tree sequesters about 50 pounds of CO_2 annually. Two acres of mature trees sequester about as much as the average American produces annually. Biodiversity: Oak trees alone support up to 2,300 species — 38 types of birds, 108 fungi, 1,178 invertebrates, 31 mammals. A single tree can provide air quality benefits worth $2/year, energy savings benefits of $7/year, and stormwater benefits of $18/year.

| CHALLENGES | Droughts. Invasive species. Animals. |

| RESOURCES | The 100+ publications by Purdue's FNR extension service, like FNR-IDNR-36 and FNR-223. U.S. Department of Agriculture's Farm Services Agency conservation programs. Nurseries: IDNR Jasper-Pulaski and Vallonia state nurseries, Woody Warehouse for potted trees, Brambleberry Permaculture Farm for fruit trees. |

| ADVICE | Plant any of Indiana's 100+ native species. Know your soil types. Plant in late March through mid-May. Learn from consulting foresters. Every county has a Department of Agriculture. Learn about cost share programs. Plant densely, like 8 × 8 ft, because only 50–80% of seedlings survive. |

Capturing All of Indiana's Emissions

CARBON SINKS

Most Hoosiers don't realize that Indiana ranks fourth in the nation for the highest carbon emissions from large stationary sources. Indiana could capture all of these emissions and store them safely underground for 300+ years.

At least that's the promise of carbon capture and storage (CCS). First, CO_2 is removed from the exhaust at a factory or power plant. Then it's compressed and injected thousands of feet underground for permanent storage. The federal government has invested over $7 billion in CCS so far. It began under Bush, and it continued with both Obama and Trump.

Kevin Ellett is a unique Hoosier. A quadfecta if you

will. He's seventh generation (from Ellettsville). A scientist (geology). Focused on climate solutions (since 2010). And an entrepreneur. He co-founded a CCS consulting firm in Bloomington, IN. "I didn't realize the severity of climate change until I lived in Australia," Kevin said. "They already had an arid climate, so it was affecting their way of life. I wanted to help. CCS feels like it's my calling."

So in 2010, he became a research scientist at IU Bloomington. He's been involved in research with over $100 million in funding and has published on topics like using CCS at Gibson Station, a coal power plant in southwestern Indiana. In 2020, he joined with Richard Middleton, PhD, formerly a senior scientist at Los Alamos National Laboratory, to create Carbon Solutions LLC.

One of their first projects is Wabash CarbonSAFE near Terre Haute, sponsored by the Department of Energy. They're working with a team led by the University of Illinois to evaluate the feasibility of capturing and storing 50 million tons or more of CO_2 emissions from a new hydrogen production plant that is in development. For context, this would be equivalent to installing solar panels on every house in Indianapolis.

Like nuclear energy from small modular reactors (SMRs), CCS could be a breakthrough that helps humanity achieve carbon neutrality. And like SMRs, we need more pilot studies and much deeper public understanding about its costs and benefits. It's too important for uninformed, emotionally charged debate.

"We need renewable energy and ways to store that energy, but that will take decades to deploy," Kevin said. "We simply don't have that kind of time. Maybe if we had started a few decades ago. CCS buys us time."

Learn More

Start with the *Carbon Storage Atlas* (5th ed.) by the DOE's National Energy Technology Laboratory (NETL). It includes impressive illustrations and in-depth explanations of pilot programs. Then see both the *National Assessment of Geologic Carbon Dioxide Storage Resources — Results* as well as *Carbon Dioxide Mineralization Feasibility in the United States* by the U.S. Geological Survey.

More Success Stories

The New Haven Tree Commission is planting **thousands of native Indiana trees** near Fort Wayne. It's using the "Miyawaki method," where forests are planted more densely which encourages rapid growth.

In Governor Eric Holcomb's 2020 State of the State address, he pledged that the Indiana Department of Natural Resources (IDNR) will plant **1 million trees in five years.** The effort is called ForestIN. At 400 trees per acre, these 2,500 acres will be enough to balance out the emissions of 1,250 Hoosiers.

Central Indiana Land Trust is planting **1 million trees over 10 years.**

In 2019, ACRES Land Trust reforested 105 acres of marginal farmland, **more than any other effort in recent history.** This includes 55,000 native hardwoods.

The 2021 American Rescue Plan earmarks **$25 million for the IDNR to acquire and preserve natural areas.** For context, the state has a mere $1 million available for these purposes from the sale of environmental license plates.

CARBON SINKS

Directory of Organizations

IDNR Classified Forest & Wildlands Program incentivizes landowners to maintain their forests with a property tax reduction, free technical assistance, and cost-sharing. bit.ly/3b8bUXm

Indiana Audubon Society protects natural resources like water, air, and soil so birds have habitat. IndianaAudubon.org

Vallonia State Nursery pays you to collect certain tree seeds throughout the state for them to plant in nurseries. They also sell seedlings. 812-358-3621

Purdue University Forestry and Natural Resources Extension Program has over 100 articles about planting trees successfully in Indiana. Purdue.edu/fnr/extension

American Indian Center of Indiana, Inc. helps the more than 55,000 American Indian and Alaskan Native people in Indiana with services ranging from employment to heritage education. When indigenous communities control their land, they can continue to protect ecosystems and manage carbon sinks. AmericanIndianCenter.org

Indiana Land Trust Protection Association is a collaboration of 24 land trusts representing 140,000 acres. ProtectIndianaLand.org See also Izaak Walton League in South Bend (IzaakSB.com) and The Nature Conservancy Indiana. TNC is the largest land trust in Indiana. Volunteer to help protect and conserve land and marine ecosystems. Nature.org

Save the Dunes protects natural areas in Northwest Indiana. SaveDunes.org

Indiana Ducks Unlimited conserves, restores, and manages wetlands so waterfowl have habitat. Linktr.ee/IndianaDucksUnlimited

Arbor Day Foundation replants trees after natural disasters with their Community Tree Recovery program, teaches students with their Tree Campus K-12 program, and offers educational materials about most tree species. ArborDay.org

Indiana Geological & Water Survey offers educational material on carbon capture and storage. IGWS.indiana.edu/sequestration

Legislation

IC 6-1.1-6 This part of the Indiana Code describes The Classified Forest and Wildlands Program. Landowners can reduce their property taxes if they follow a professionally written land management plan. Landowners also receive free assistance from foresters and wildlife biologists as well as cost-share on forest management. Minimum land required is 10 acres.

HEA 1209 Carbon sequestration projects. Provides a regulatory framework for carbon capture and storage. Also addresses pore space (the liquid or gas portions of soil) ownership, mineral rights, and long-term liability. Does not give any company blanket immunity as a related bill might have.

Enabling Conditions

"You never change things by fighting
the existing reality. To change
something, build a new model that
makes the existing model obsolete."

— *Buckminster Fuller*

OVERVIEW

Enabling conditions multiply the impact of the other Drawdown climate solutions through education, community building, and carbon pricing.

Climate action begins with education. We need to increase awareness of the goal — global carbon neutrality by 2050 — and the solutions to achieve it. This is where Project Drawdown shines. Next, we need to foster collaboration between individual actors to build momentum. They exist throughout Indiana, but are disconnected and may feel alone. Finally, we need what's called a "price on carbon," which removes incentives to pollute and makes low-carbon business models more competitive. Economists agree that the most cost effective way to achieve carbon neutrality is a free market that properly prices externalities.

Here's a little known story about Indiana. Andrew Carnegie was one of the wealthiest people of his day. He gave away almost all his money, for example, to build libraries. But there were two catches. First, a community needed to donate the land. Next, they needed to tax themselves in perpetuity to maintain it. Indiana has more Carnegie libraries than any other state, meaning that we rallied to invest in knowledge and the next generation. We can also be proud of environmental reporting by the *IndyStar* and the *Indiana Environmental Reporter*. And have you heard of Gene Stratton-Porter? She was a Hoosier environmental writer. According to *Smithsonian Magazine*, she was "as famous in the early 1900s as J.K. Rowling is now." Her novels reached 50 million readers in more than 20 languages.

DRAWDOWN SOLUTIONS

Education
Community-building
Carbon pricing

These solutions enable all others, and were not part of the original Project Drawdown calculations.

Climate-Themed Little Free Libraries

"I read so much as a kid," Ethan Bledsoe said. "I'd spend the entire day reading. We had an Accelerated Reader program at school, with points awarded for each book completed, and I wanted to win."

Ethan was lucky enough to grow up in a college town. Still, he didn't learn about climate change until a chance encounter during the Science Olympiad competition.

"I was shocked. If global warming is such a serious problem, why didn't I learn about it in school earlier?"

Ethan said he and his friends realized the City of West Lafayette "wasn't doing anything about [it]. There was a lot of talk but nothing was being done."

So in May 2019, they founded West Lafayette Climate. The group organized five climate strikes, created a youth position on the City Council, passed a climate resolution, got Lafayette to create a climate action plan, and even launched a statewide campaign called Confront the Climate Crisis.

"But then I realized we were only targeting other high-schoolers, not younger kids. What if we distributed books for multiple age levels, like picture books?"

They received a $1,500 Service Learning Grant from Purdue University. With the money, they built seven Little Free Libraries. These sit on posts in peoples' front yards and look like bird houses. Anyone can take a book or leave a book. Ethan's group filled them with books about climate.

"Our motto became 'climate literacy is climate resiliency,'" Ethan said.

Now this bright, caring young man is leaving Indiana to attend university in Chicago, but he leaves behind at least two incredible legacies. The climate group has new leadership to carry on the torch — and the libraries will shine the light of knowledge for the next generation.

Can I Do This?

COSTS

$25 if you build your own, $250 if you buy pre-made. $100 for used books. Started in December, got grants in March, libraries installed by April. Building and painting took 15 people 2–3 hours each. Installing took 20 people.

BENEFITS

More education leads to more action. Little Free Libraries are a low-cost way to plant seeds of knowledge. They require time to build, but only a little time to maintain.

PROCESS

Decide where the library will be. Pick a place with foot traffic. → Identify a long-term caretaker. → Build or buy a library from **LittleFreeLibrary.org/start** → Consider registering the library and creating a steward account. → Fill with books. → Celebrate, host a grand opening, invite local media.

ADVICE

Consider repurposing old kitchen cabinets. Buy used books from Better World Books, an Indiana company. Build large enough for picture books. Select books for all ages. Make sure to weatherize the library: **bit.ly/3Q1FR66** More advice: **bit.ly/3xL9mqI**

SUGGESTED BOOKS

Earth Remembers When by Dawn Wynne

Linus the Vegetarian T-Rex by Robert Neubecker

Hope in the Dark by Rebecca Solnit

The Lorax by Dr. Seuss

No Green Eggs or Ham by Flora Lee

Earth from Above by Yann Arthus-Bertrand

Dreaming in Turtle by Peter Laufer

Dire Predictions by Lee Kump and Michael E. Mann

Silent Spring by Rachel Carson

An Inconvenient Truth by Al Gore

Saving Us by Katharine Hayhoe

Drawdown by Paul Hawken

Regeneration by Paul Hawken

Carbon Neutral Indiana by Daniel S. Poynter

Mother Nurtures Environmental Community

"Can you speak to the television news station?" It was a sunny day, and Addie's newborn was snug in her baby sling as she walked around answering questions.

There were over 2,000 people at Eco Fest Fort Wayne. Vendors were selling goods and teaching about recycling, native plants, rain barrels, urban forests, land trusts, and pollinator habitats. Hundreds of passionate people, each committed to improving their city.

After graduating from college in sports management, Addie Farris coached gymnastics, helped her mother run an antique store, and helped her husband expand his business in Toledo, Ohio.

She gave birth to her child. "I was already doing the best I could to live sustainably," she said. "When my son was born I wondered about everyone else. How could I help them learn? And how could we grow a community to help each other?"

That's when she connected with the Toledo Lucas County Sustainability Commission. She heard about an Eco Fest in Jackson Hole, Wyoming, and decided to pitch the idea to the

Toledo commission. By investing 10 hours per week for a few months, she convinced local groups to purchase booth space. That first Eco Fest in Toledo cost about $1,200, and over a thousand people came.

So when she moved back to Fort Wayne, Addie just had to organize another one. As the event grew, more companies paid to sponsor it, and she invested that money into advertising. Now it's a standalone nonprofit that's taken root in Fort Wayne. "Our mission is to highlight the organizations in our community that are pushing sustainability forward," Addie said.

ECO FESTIVAL EVENT

Can I Do This?

COSTS

Biggest costs are venue, event insurance, and advertising. Roughly $1,300 in the first year. Unpaid labor. First two years, all profits went into the event.

BENEFITS

Nurture community. Educate. Inspire.

PROCESS

1 Decide: will the event be indoors or outdoors? During which season? **2** Select venue. Do they provide chairs, tables, tents? **3** Decide price for food, vendor, and nonprofit booths. Consider discounts for early registration.
4 Set a goal for vendors; 30–50 the first year is a good start. **5** Create promotional material like a postcard. **6** Ask businesses to sponsor the event and give them promo materials.
7 Make a list of larger companies to approach about sponsorships. Ask friends and family who they know there. **8** Invite the media to cover the event. **9** Have attendees provide feedback.

Credibility. The first year you'll need to hustle more to prove yourself to all participants. Later the event will sell itself. Delegation. You can start it by yourself, but you'll need a team to grow.

Make communication with vendors organized and detailed. They appreciate this. Sustainability is for everyone. Don't assume some types of people won't engage.

The Most Powerful Climate Solution of All

What do Elon Musk and most Republicans under 40 agree on? Carbon pricing. It respects the free market and promotes innovation.

Heather Swinney grew up in New Albany, a small town on the Ohio River. As a kid, she loved riding her bike. She rode it to the general store and bought sandwiches for just 50 cents. Eventually she moved away. She earned her degree and taught English for over a decade.

But when it came time to start her family, Heather moved back home to Indiana.

"Becoming a stay-at-home mom gave me a little more time to think about the environment," Heather said. "And for me, climate is the core environmental problem."

There wasn't much going on in southern Indiana, so she joined organizations across the river in Louisville. That's when she discovered Citizens' Climate Lobby (CCL). They promote a straightforward, bipartisan policy.

First, the government places a fee on fossil fuels when they enter the economy. The fee is assessed at the oil well, coal mine, or port. Then that fee is distributed back to every

American as a dividend. This incentivizes a transition to clean energy — without making the government bigger.

Heather decided to start a CCL chapter in New Albany. First, she found a mentor from another chapter. Then she hosted a kick-off event and monthly meetings at the library. A few years later, 10–15 people participate regularly, and her team helped convince the first Indiana Representative to sign on as a co-sponsor to a carbon fee-and-dividend bill in Congress.

"What I like about CCL is that we don't focus on the problem. We focus on a solution. And to me a carbon fee-and-dividend is a very effective solution."

CITIZENS' CLIMATE LOBBY

Can I Do This?

COSTS

Printing fliers. Paying to table at events. Possibly renting a meeting room. Two hours/week at the beginning, less if other co-founders are helping.

BENEFITS

"Everything about this is fun," Heather said. "The excitement of creating something new. The robust educational resources CCL provides."

PROCESS

1 Find a CCL group nearby. There are many throughout Indiana. **2** Ask for veterans to mentor you. **3** Understand the goal of the group clearly: to pass climate solution legislation at the federal level. **4** Make sure everyone in your life knows about the group (friends, neighbors, faith organizations, Master Gardeners program, etc.) **5** Hold an event with free food and drinks, or a movie showing. **6** Table at a farmer's market every week.

Sometimes it's easy to get lost in the weeds. Remember the big picture.

Indiana has 12 local CCL chapters. Find them at `CitizensClimateLobby.org`

Have a plan for involving new people. Who follows up with them? What's their role? Make them feel welcomed and included. The best way to grow is one-on-one conversations with neighbors, friends. Be ready for things not to go according to plan. Roll with it.

Michigan City Creates Emissions Baseline

"When birds sat on their eggs to brood," Nancy said, "those eggs broke. The pesticide DDT made the shells too thin. The baby birds didn't have a chance. I read this as a teen and cried."

The book *Silent Spring* by Rachel Carson changed Nancy Moldenhauer's life forever. She became president of her high school's Earth Club. Then she learned that the local power plant's expansion was going to dump hot water into Lake Michigan. This would kill fish and grow algae. So her club circulated a petition and got thousands of signatures. As a result, the plant installed a water cooling tower. This was just the beginning. Nancy would become one of Indiana's most persistent advocates for community and environmental health.

Decades later, the nonprofit Earth Charter Indiana hosted a gathering of mayors to discuss climate change. Nancy and a few other community members attended, and came back inspired. Six of them decided to create the Michigan City Sustainability Commission (MCSC). "It's not an advisory committee," Nancy said. "It's a legal entity of the City. Mayors come and go, but they can't get rid of us." For context, this was three years before Indianapolis created a similar group, and Indy's city budget is 25 times larger.

Many of the MCSC commissioners have become carbon neutral through Carbon Neutral Indiana. They've helped install solar panels and earned national recognition with a SolSmart silver designation. They also conducted a greenhouse gas inventory to learn where the city's carbon emissions come from.

In 2019, Nancy helped Michigan City join Indiana University's Resilience Cohort, hosted by the Environmental Resilience Institute. Abhishek Jagdale, a graduate student, visited for the summer to collect data on electricity, natural gas, waste water, solid waste, and more. "Our biggest challenge," Nancy said, "was people didn't know what a greenhouse gas inventory was. We learned that our waste emissions are disproportionately large."

Nancy's work struck a chord. A friend of hers, Kathy Sipple, formed NWI Region Resilience, expanding the idea to include all of Northwest Indiana. Lake, Porter, and LaPorte counties — and dozens of cities — joined together and created a carbon inventory for the entire region. Northwestern Indiana Regional Planning Commission is creating a plan for the entire area, similar to the Resilience Action Plan that Michigan City Sustainability Commission created.

"There might only be two other places in the country that have made a regional plan like this," Nancy said. "Persistence is so important. Never give up when you believe you can improve the health, well-being, and quality of life for the people around you. Never give up. Keep going until you reach that ideal."

Can I Do This?

CHALLENGES

Nancy has dyslexia. "Figure out how to get around challenges, move beyond them."

ADVICE

Inspire younger leaders around you. Know what motivates people, what their interests are, what makes them happy. Guide them to ignore obstacles. Let them take the actions.

More Success Stories

EDUCATION

Indiana University-Purdue University Indianapolis ranks **second in the U.S. for sustainability.** Rankings are based on the United Nations Sustainable Development Goals.

C-SPAN has been educating television audiences about **civics since 1979.** Programming includes interviews with non-fiction authors and individuals associated with public policy. Founder Brian Lamb is from Lafayette.

Eight cities in Indiana joined Climate Mayors, a bipartisan network of 470 majors implementing climate action in their communities. Cities include Bloomington, Carmel, Evansville, Fort Wayne, Gary, Indianapolis, South Bend, West Lafayette. ClimateMayors.org

COMMUNITY-BUILDING

Two Indiana lawmakers joined the Conservative Climate Caucus in the U.S. House of Representatives, Rep. Jim Baird and Rep. Larry Bucshon.

ENABLING CONDITIONS

Indiana Senator Mike Braun co-created the bipartisan Climate Solutions Caucus with Sen. Chris Coons of Delaware.

Indiana is the only state with a community foundation in every county. This existing infrastructure could help implement local climate solutions.

Community Development Financial Institutions provide financial services to communities that lack such access. Bloomington is the first "CDFI Friendly" city in the nation, which will leverage local and national investment.

CARBON PRICING

50 professional economists from Indiana universities signed a letter calling for a price on carbon. Universities include Purdue University, Indiana University and the University of Notre Dame.

Rep. André Carson (IN-07) became the 84th co-sponsor of H.R. 763, the Energy Innovation and Carbon Dividend Act. This is the bill advocated for by Citizens' Climate Lobby. It puts a fee on carbon and returns the revenue to households.

Directory of Organizations

EDUCATION

Carbon Neutral Indiana
can measure your household's footprint for free. Join a community of over 200 Hoosiers who balance out their emissions by buying carbon offsets. They also educate Hoosiers by sponsoring climate solutions journalism at universities and by publishing this book.
CarbonNeutralIndiana.org

Earth Charter Indiana
hosts climate summer camps for youth, helps people pass climate ordinances in their towns, and manages the Indiana Thriving Schools Challenge. Schools implement gardens, reduce energy use and waste, and implement climate curriculum.
EarthCharterIndiana.org

Hoosier Environmental Council educates and organizes on environmental topics generally, including renewable energy, protecting wilderness areas, and reducing pollution. `HECweb.org`

Purdue Climate Change Research Center is Purdue's hub for all climate education. Changing name soon to the Purdue Institute for Climate, Environment, Food, and Sustainability. `Ag.purdue.edu/climate` See also Midwestern Regional Climate Center, hosted at Purdue. `MRCC.purdue.edu`

Green Voters Guide provides candidate views on climate-related policies. `VotersForAGreenIndiana.org.` See also Carmel Green Initiative, which contributes articles to the Carmel Current and hosts film screenings. `CarmelGreen.org`

Indiana University's Environmental Resilience Institute is IU's hub for all climate education. They can help you measure your city's carbon emissions, create a climate action plan, and reduce emissions. `ERI.iu.edu`

COMMUNITY-BUILDING

Eco Fest Fort Wayne is an annual event in Fort Wayne promoting small businesses that care about the environment. `EcoFestFW.com` See also Earth Day Indiana, an annual event in Indianapolis. `EarthDayIndiana.org`

Elders Climate Action connects you with a community of seniors to advocate for effective climate public policy. Their current project encourages all Indiana utilities to use 100% clean energy by 2040. `EldersClimateAction.org`

Creation Care Ministry of the Archdiocese of Indianapolis provides education to Central and Southern Indiana. See also Indiana Catholics for Creation, a statewide group of lay people and priests working together to protect our common home. `OurCommonHome.org`

The Evangelical Environmental Network equips, educates, and mobilizes evangelical Christians to love God and others by rediscovering and reclaiming the Biblical mandate to care for creation. `CreationCare.org`

Directory continues on next page.

ENABLING CONDITIONS

Faith in Place mobilizes faith communities to respond to global warming. Formerly Hoosier Interfaith Power and Light. Now includes Indiana, Wisconsin, Illinois. `FaithInPlace.org`. See also Tri-State Creation Care, which hosts meetings for faith communities focused on creation care. Many members are in Evansville, IN. `Facebook.com/TriStateCreationCare`

CARBON PRICING

Citizens' Climate Lobby advocates for carbon pricing. `CitizensClimateLobby.org`. See also Hoosiers for Carbon Dividends, a conservative-based organization advocating for carbon pricing. `HoosierCarbonDividends.org`

Legislation

Energy Innovation and Carbon Dividend Act. The most broadly supported carbon pricing bill in Congress. Promoted by Citizens' Climate Lobby. H.R. 2307 includes a revenue neutral fee-and-dividend solution where most of the money collected is returned to households as a dividend.

America's Clean Future Fund Act. Promoted by Sen. Durbin (D-IL). Includes carbon pricing, but only 75% of revenue would be returned to households as dividends.

Save Our Future Act. Promoted by Sen. Whitehouse (D-RI) and Sen. Schatz (D-HI). Combines a carbon price with a price on air pollutants more generally.

Climate Action Rebate Act. Promoted by Sen. Coons (D-DE) and Sen. Feinstein (D-CA). A carbon price, but only 70% of revenue is returned to households.

MARKET CHOICE Act. Promoted by Rep. Fitzpatrick (R-PA), Rep. Peters (D-CA), and Rep. Carbajal (D-CA). An infrastructure bill that includes funding from a carbon price.

45Q. Federal tax law that provides a tax credit to power plants and industrial facilities when they capture and store CO_2.

Conclusion

The best way to end this book is not with more words but with action. So what's next? Everyone loves checklists! So if you only do **ONE** thing next, let it be this:

○ Let me know what you thought. I can use your feedback to improve the next edition. `CarbonNeutralIndiana.org/book-feedback`

And if you are willing to do **THREE** more things:

○ Deepen your comprehension of the material in this book by completing the crossword puzzle. You can even win a prize when you do.

○ Measure your household's carbon footprint for free at `CarbonNeutralIndiana.org`

○ This book is just the beginning. Follow us on social media to stay in the loop for future projects. `CarbonNeutralIndiana.org/book`

And if you are willing to do **TEN** more things:

○ Know a story, organization, or piece of legislation to be included in the next book? Submit it here: `CarbonNeutralIndiana.org/book`

○ Cover the cost of distributing these books to more leaders throughout Indiana. Contribute at `CarbonNeutralIndiana.org/donate`

○ Write an email to anyone profiled in this book, and thank them for what they're doing. Your encouragement will fuel them.

○ Attend one Citizens' Climate Lobby meeting in your area. `CitizensClimateLobby.org`

○ Attend a Solar 101 event near you: `SolarUnitedNeighbors.org`

○ Watch one of these documentaries: *Kiss the Ground*, *Merchants of Doubt*, or *Forks Over Knives*.

○ Listen to one episode of this podcast: `MCJCollective.com`

○ Subscribe to this email newsletter: `Centered.tech`

○ Make sure you're using all LED bulbs in your home.

○ Find an insulation expert who can measure your home's "building envelope." `Angi.com`

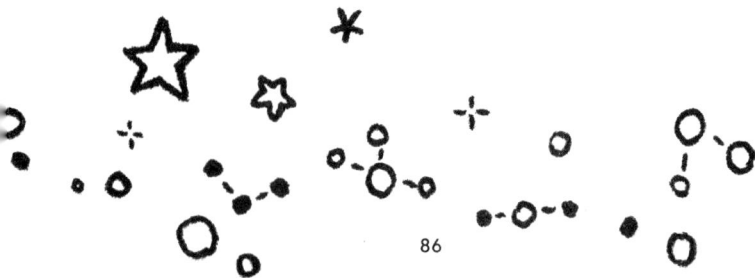

Appendix

More Resources

Project Drawdown | Book and website listing the most cost effective ways to reduce carbon emissions globally. Created by hundreds of PhDs. `Drawdown.com`

Global Weirding: Climate, Politics, and Religion with Katharine Hayhoe | Short videos explaining climate change. Dr. Hayhoe is an atmospheric scientist, evangelical Christian, and Chief Scientist of the Nature Conservancy.
`PBS.org/show/global-weirding`

EPA Greenhouse Gas (GHG) Emissions and Removals
Authoritative crash course. Also see their report *Inventory of U.S. Greenhouse Gas Emissions and Sinks: 1990-2020.*
`EPA.gov/ghgemissions`

EPA GHG Reporting Program | Map of the largest carbon emitters in the U.S. `EPA.gov/ghgreporting`

Indiana Climate Change Impacts Assessment
A series of reports showing how climate change will affect Indiana infrastructure, agriculture, tourism and recreation, forests, health, and more. Created by 100+ experts from Purdue, Notre Dame, Ball State, Indiana University, and more.
`Ag.purdue.edu/indianaclimate`

Implications of Climate Change for the U.S. Army **(2019)**
Report commissioned by the Pentagon. It describes how the military could collapse because of pressures from climate migration, drought, flooding.

My Climate Journey | Podcast. A former technology entrepreneur interviews people in the climate innovation pipeline: scientists, engineers, entrepreneurs, investors, policymakers, nonprofit leaders. `MCJCollective.com`

Centered | A daily email newsletter by Katie Pyzyk highlighting cleantech news throughout the Midwest. `Centered.tech`

Terra.do | Want to change careers and work on climate full-time? Pay for a crash course from top climate experts. Use their job board to find your next climate job. `Terra.do`

Climate Base | Another job board with thousands of opportunities to work on climate. `ClimateBase.org`

Work On Climate | A large Slack community full of people who want to work on climate full-time. Many former employees from Facebook, Google, Apple. Lists jobs available and other resources. `WorkOnClimate.org`

Pique Action | Very short, professionally made videos about cutting-edge climate solutions. `PiqueAction.com`

Apocalypse Never: Why Environmental Alarmism Hurts Us All (2020) | By longtime environmental activist Michael Shellenberger. Distinguishes reasonable concern from apocalyptic environmentalism. Shows how technology can ease pressure on ecosystems, like how plastic replaced demand for turtle shells.

Breakthrough Institute | Environmental think tank founded by Michael Shellenberger and Ted Nordhaus. Promotes economic and technological development. `TheBreakThrough.org`

Electric Municipal Utilities and the Transition to a Clean Energy Future: A Guide for Municipal Utility Leaders (2022) Published by the nonprofit Climate Cabinet. See also their *Rural Electric Cooperatives and the Transition to a Clean Energy Future: A Guide for Cooperative Leaders.* `ClimateCabinetEducation.org`

"Leverage Points: Places to Intervene in a System" Short essay by Donella Meadows. Essential reading. Describes how to accomplish a lot with a little.

Cradle to Cradle | Classic book by William McDonough that inspires many in the circular economy movement.

Group Discussion Questions

GENERAL

▸ What are your favorite childhood memories of growing up in Indiana?

▸ What do you think of the Warren Buffet quote in the preface?

▸ Do you know people who despair about climate change? What's their core reason for doing so?

▸ Which success stories surprised you most? Why do you think these stories aren't widely known?

▸ Which of the climate solutions could you implement in a weekend? In a month? In a year?

▸ Have you measured your carbon footprint with Carbon Neutral Indiana? What did you learn?

▸ What do you want to remember from this book?

1 ELECTRICITY

▸ Which buildings do you use throughout the month? How might they become more energy-efficient?

▸ What's preventing more hydropower in Indiana?

▸ What are all of the risks and benefits you can name about small modular nuclear power?

▸ Does your school district have solar power yet?

2 FOOD, AGRICULTURE & LAND USE

- ‣ Have you ever composted food waste?

- ‣ Have you seen the film *Kiss the Ground* yet? What did you think?

- ‣ Have you experimented with a plant-rich lifestyle for a period of time? What was it like?

3 INDUSTRY

- ‣ Did you realize manufacturing is so much bigger in Indiana than agriculture?

- ‣ Do you know any children who compete in robotics?

- ‣ Will you need to remove trees on your property soon?

4 TRANSPORTATION & BUILDINGS

- ‣ Does your school district have an electric bus?

- ‣ How does your city limit new gas stations?

- ‣ Have you driven an electric vehicle? What was it like?

- ‣ How much money and time do you spend commuting to work?

5 CARBON SINKS

- Have you ever planted a tree? What was it like? Is it still around? Have you ever helped a child plant one?

- What's your favorite memory of a forest? Why is it worth remembering? What did it smell like? Where do you feel the memory in your body?

- Have you ever donated to a land trust? Which one?

- What questions do you have about carbon capture and storage (CCS)?

6 ENABLING CONDITIONS

- What sources in your life provide helpful knowledge about climate change? How do you support those sources?

- Where could you install a climate-themed Little Free Library in your town? What would you put in it?

- Have you ever been in a Carnegie library?

- Have you been to a CCL meeting? What was it like?

- Have you ever read the *IndyStar*'s environmental reporting? Or anything from the *Indiana Environmental Reporter*?

- Questions drive learning. What questions do you have about climate change? About reducing emissions? About adapting to coming environmental changes?

Crossword Puzzle

2 Could power 500,000 homes in Indiana.

7 Indiana produces more of this than any other state.

8 Solution ___ .

9 Responsible for 8% of all global emissions.

12 List of most effective climate solutions.

13 Largest group of scientists in history.

16 Leading Indiana manufacturer of geothermal systems.

18 Economy when materials are reused.

19 First to run a four-minute mile.

21 Dying as the ocean becomes more acidic.

D O W N

1 Could be 7,000 times worse than carbon dioxide.

3 Annual event promoting plant-rich lifestyles.

4 Covey's favorite circle.

5 First electric streetlights.

6 Published by DOE's NETL. On 5th edition.

10 Climate solution that economists love. Carbon ___ .

11 Over ___ % of Hoosiers are worried about climate change.

14 Balancing carbon emissions with removals.

15 Conservative quoted in this book.

17 Can help reduce cow methane 30%.

20 Growing Climate Solutions Act.

ENTER TO WIN!

Finish the crossword puzzle? Take a photo of it. Then scan this QR code to upload the photo. You might win a prize.

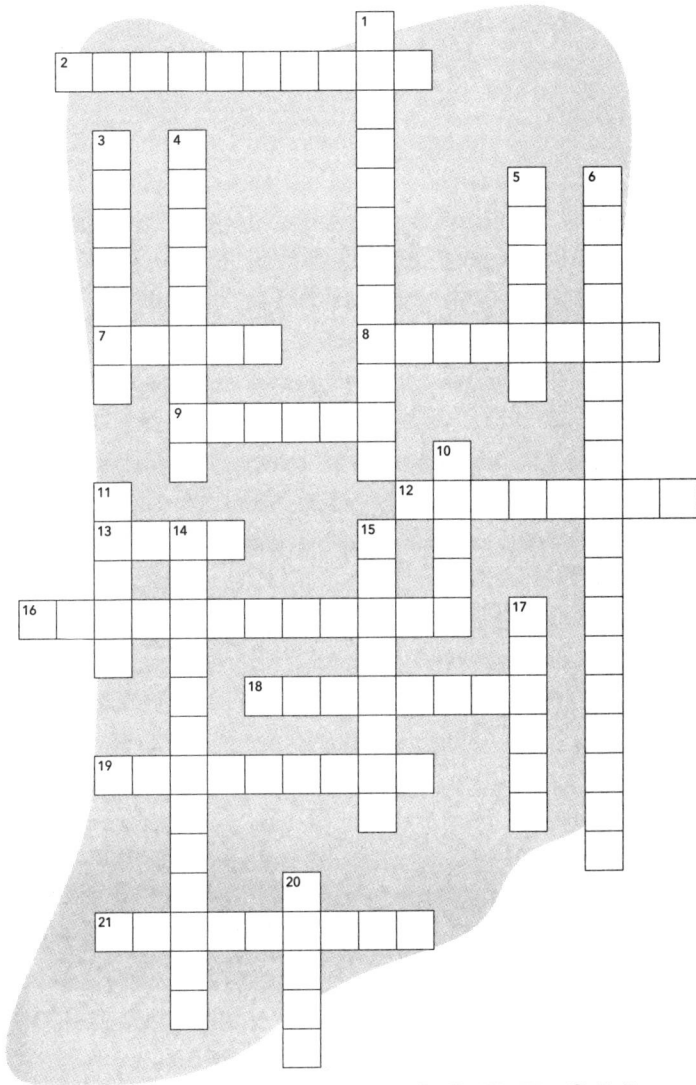

CARBON NEUTRAL INDIANA

Index

ACRES Land Trust 67

AlGalCo 26

American Institute of Architects 59

American Society of Heating, Refrigerating
and Air-Conditioning Engineers 59

An Inconvenient Truth 75

Ashley 45

Association of Indiana Solid Waste Management Districts 46

Baird, Jim 81

Ball State University 12, 18, 56, 87

Ballard, Greg 11, 40

Bargersville 58

Bike Indianapolis 59

Bledsoe, Ethan 11, 73

Bloomington 11, 13, 21, 22, 27, 45, 46, 66, 81, 82

Brand, Stewart 10

Braun, Mike 11, 38, 82

Brightmark 45

Bucshon, Larry 81

Buffet, Warren 8

Building efficiency 18, 21, 22, 47, 50

Bush, George H. W. 15

Bush, George W. 15

Carbon neutral 14, 45, 66, 72, 80, 82

Carbon Neutral Indiana 8, 9, 11, 75, 80, 82, 89

Carbon price 77, 84

Carbon sinks 61, 62, 91

Carmel 13, 26, 53, 81, 83

Carnegie, Andrew 72

Carson, André 82

Carson, Rachel 75, 79

Cement 40, 41, 45, 62

Central Indiana Land Trust 67

Central Indiana Regional Transportation Authority 59

China 31

Circular economy 40, 43, 46, 88

Circular Indiana 12, 46

Citizens Action Coalition 28

Citizens' Climate Lobby 11, 12, 13, 77, 78, 82, 84, 86

Clemens, Lauren 11, 21

Climate polling.. 16

Community & Environmental Defense Services. 53

Community Development Financial Institutions 21, 82

Confidence 14

Conservation Cropping Systems Initiative of Indiana 38

Conservatives for a Clean Energy Future 27

Coral reef 8

Covey, Stephen 14, 92

Cultivate Food Rescue. 36, 37

Daniels, Mitch 18

Danville 45

Democracy 16

Department of Energy 22, 58, 66

Dick, Gerry. 10

Diet for a New America 34

Dire Predictions 75

Ditzler, Will 11, 63

Doral Renewable Energy Group 26

Dreaming in Turtle. 75

Drive Clean Indiana. 59

Dun Agro Hemp Group, Inc. 45

Earth Charter Indiana 13, 36, 79, 82

Earth from Above. 74

Earth Remembers When 74

Edison, Thomas 39

Electric vehicles 50, 54, 55, 57, 59, 60, 90

Ellett, Kevin. 11, 65

Ellettsville 66

Emegoakor, Chisom. 58

ENERGY STAR 21, 59

Energy Systems Network. 13, 28

Evansville. 27, 42, 81, 84

Farming 32, 33, 38

Farris, Addie. 10, 11, 75

Fasick, Doug 12, 41

Feltman, Nate 10

Folds, Ben 49

Food waste 32, 36, 37, 46, 62, 90

Ford, Henry 39

Fort Wayne 8, 26, 41, 42, 45, 46, 67, 75, 76, 81, 83

Franklin County Community School Corporation....................24
Fuller, Buckminster 71
Gary..81
Gibson, John 10
Gigatons...15
Greater Indiana Clean Cities, Inc. 12, 59
Greensburg...23
Grind2Energy...36
Growing Climate Solutions Act......................................38
Hamilton Heights School Corporation 33
Hawken, Paul..10, 61, 75
Henry, Tom 42
Hipskind, Kelly 12, 23
Historic buildings...56
Hobart...23
Holcomb, Eric..67
Hoosier Electric Vehicles Association 59
Hope in The Dark 74
Huntington...12, 13, 42, 56
Hurt, Larry..43
HVAC...50
Hydropower...19, 29, 89
Indiana Agriculture Nutrient Alliance Inc. 38
Indiana Association of Soil and Water Conservation Districts.......38
Indiana Conservative Alliance for Energy......................11, 28
Indiana Department of Natural Resources...................65, 67, 68
Indiana Department of Transportation 50, 57
Indiana General Assembly 15
Indiana Geothermal...28
Indiana Land Trust Protection Association 68
Indiana Solar for All..28
Indiana University.................12, 47, 56, 63, 80, 82, 83, 87
Indiana Wesleyan University..24
Indianapolis 37, 40, 42, 43, 44, 46, 50, 58, 59, 66, 80, 81, 83
Indianapolis 500 37
Indianapolis Business Journal....................................10
Indianapolis International Airport.........................8, 26, 50
Indianapolis Public Schools....................................24, 58
Indy Urban Hardwood Co. 13, 44
Indy VegFest...34, 35, 37
Inside INdiana Business..10

International Ground Source Heat Pump Association 28
IPCC 14
Jagdale, Abhishek 80
K12 Food Rescue 33, 36, 37
Keplinger, Bryn 12, 56
Kinetrex Energy 45
Kirk, Dana 43
Knox 18, 26
Kramer, Robert 37
Linus the Vegetarian T-Rex 74
Little Free Libraries 73, 74, 91
Local Harvest 37
Manufacturing 40, 45, 47, 90
Maurer, Mickey 10, 12
Menon, Kumar 42
Michigan City 12, 19, 20, 79, 80
Middleton, Richard 66
Moldenhauer, Nancy 10, 12, 79, 80
Momentum 14, 72
Monticello 45
Moore, Faye 12, 19
Moran, Richard 43
MPS Egg Farms 45
Mudawar, Issam 57
Musk, Elon 77
NAACP 19, 27
National Energy Technology Laboratory 67
Negele, Sharon 27
Net-zero 14, 59
New Albany 77, 78
Newfields 44
New Haven 67
No Green Eggs or Ham 74
Noblesville 33
Notre Dame University 24, 26, 36, 58, 82, 87
Nuclear power 18, 19, 26, 29, 66, 89
Oak Ridge National Laboratory 26
Phillips, Jackie 13, 51
Poer, Patrick 24
Portage 23
Poynter, Cait 5, 10

Poynter, Daniel..9, 75, 100

Presnell, Brian...13, 43

Project Drawdown................. 10, 14, 15, 18, 32, 40, 50, 62, 72, 87

Purdue University 8, 10, 12, 13, 18, 26, 32, 37, 41, 45, 50
57, 58, 68, 73, 82, 83, 87, 100

Pyzyk, Katie..10, 88

Reagan, Ronald 15

RecycleForce 46

ReFED 34, 37

Refrigerants 41, 46, 50

Regeneration...75

Remora Carbon 58

Richard G. Lugar Center for Renewable Energy.....................28

Rowling, J.K..72

Rupp, Katelin 34

Saving Us 75

School buses...18, 27, 57

Shock, Audra..13, 33

Silent Spring 75, 79

Sipple, Kathy..80

Smith, Terry...27

Solar energy 19, 24, 27, 28, 30

Solar United Neighbors 19, 21, 27

Solarize Indiana 27

Solution aversion 15

Sortera Alloys...45

South Bend..21, 22, 68, 81

Starch...31

Steel 40, 45

Steel Dynamics..45

Stratton-Porter, Gene..................................72

Sun FundED 12, 24, 27

Swinney, Heather......................................13, 77

Taylor University 24

Terre Haute...46, 66

Tesla, Nikola..17

Thatcher, Margaret 15

The 7 Habits of Highly Effective People 14

The Food Architect 37

The Heritage Group 40

The Lorax 74

The Nature Conservancy 64, 68, 87

U.S. Geological Survey 67

U.S. Green Building Council 60

University of Indianapolis 36

Velay-Lizancos, Mirian 45

Wabash 18

Wabash Valley Resources 40

WaterFurnace 26

West Clay 51

West Lafayette 42, 46, 73

White paint 56, 58

Whited, Kevin 13, 53

Whitehead, Don 63

Whole Earth Catalog 10

Wilcox, Michael 26

Williamson, John 33

Winnecke, Lloyd 27

Wood 32, 43, 44, 45, 67

Wyatt 45

About the Author

DANIEL SCOTT POYNTER founded Carbon Neutral Indiana. With a wide variety of supporters, CNI is growing a nonpartisan, grassroots community that is helping the state reduce and balance out its carbon emissions. It's rooted in the understanding that with free minds and free markets, humanity's best days are yet to come.

Daniel grew up in Indiana, studied philosophy at Purdue University, and was named a MacArthur Foundation Young Innovator. Before starting CNI, he was a software engineer and advisor to over 100 entrepreneurs. Daniel is a direct, matrilineal descendent of Patrick "give me liberty or give me death!" Henry.

You can reach Daniel at `dpoynter@carbonneutralindiana.org`.

About the Artists

RACHEL LEIGH is a multidisciplinary designer of educational guides and videos. Her images, words, and sounds create spaces of aesthetic focus that support the curious, engaged learners inside all of us. Find her work at Majuscule.co.

BRANDON SCHAAF is a designer and animator who thrives on shared vision. Whether collaboratively or independently, you'll find him working to uplift, inspire, and entertain. Scroll through a portfolio at BrandonSchaaf.com